hope and the future

Also by Charles Johnston:

The Creative Imperative: Human Growth and Planetary Evolution

Necessary Wisdom: Meeting the Challenge of a New Cultural Maturity

Pattern and Reality: A Brief Introduction to Creative Systems Theory

The Power of Diversity: An Introduction to the Creative Systems Personality Typology

An Evolutionary History of Music: Introducing Creative Systems Theory Through the Language of Sound (DVD)

Cultural Maturity: A Guidebook for the Future (with an Introduction to the Ideas of Creative Systems Theory)

Quick and Dirty Answers to the Biggest of Questions: Creative Systems Theory Explains What It Is All About (Really)

Online:

The Institute for Creative Development: www.CreativeSystems.org

Cultural Maturity-A Blog for the Future: www.CulturalMaturityBlog.net

Creative Systems Theory: www.CSTHome.org

Cultural Maturity: www.CulturalMaturity.org

The Creative Systems Personality Typology: www.CSPTHome.org

hope
and the future

An Introduction to the
Concept of Cultural Maturity

Charles M. Johnston, MD

The Institute for Creative Development (ICD) Press
Seattle, Washington

Cover design by Les Campbell

Author photo by Brad Kevelin

Library of Congress Control Number: 2013918893

First printing 2014

hope and the future

BACKGROUND

This volume is one of three related works I have released at about the same time with similar intent: to help people understand the times we live in and to make sense of what the future will require of us as a species. Each book is written for a different audience.

Hope and the Future is the introductory book in this series. It describes how our times present challenges that require new human skills and capacities, and introduces the critical cultural "growing up" on which our future depends. It is intended for a general audience wanting to better understand the tasks humanity now faces.

Cultural Maturity: A Guidebook for the Future (with an Introduction to the Ideas of Creative Systems Theory) presents a more detailed examination of these new skills and capacities with specific emphasis given to the new kinds of understanding that they necessarily draw on. It is a longer work written for those interested in developing the newly sophisticated leadership abilities that we will increasingly need in all parts of our lives.[1]

The third book in the series, *Quick and Dirty Answers to the Biggest of Questions,* describes how the new kind of understanding we need today, besides helping us address modern-day challenges, also brings a new maturity and creativity of perspective to more ultimate sorts of questions. It is a more theoretical work intended for people who find particular fascination in overarching inquiry.[2]

---

1 Johnston, Charles, *Cultural Maturity: A Guidebook for the Future,* ICD Press, 2015

2 Johnston, Charles, *Quick and Dirty Answers to the Biggest of Questions: Creative Systems Theory Explains What It is All About (Really),* ICD Press, 2013

The thinking in these books has its origins in the ideas of Creative Systems Theory (CST), a comprehensive framework for understanding change, interrelationship, and purpose in human systems that I first introduced more than thirty years ago and later refined with colleagues at the Institute for Creative Development.[3] The theory is significant both for the practical usefulness of its ideas and for the kind of thinking that it represents. Creative Systems Theory itself is an example of the new kind of understanding that we will increasingly need in times ahead.

—Charles Johnston

---

3   Creative Systems Theory was first described in written form in my 1984 book *The Creative Imperative*. (See Johnston, Charles, *The Creative Imperative: Human Growth and Planetary Evolution*, Celestial Arts, 1984.) The Institute for Creative Development is a Seattle-based think tank and center for advanced leadership training. (See www.CreativeSystems.org.)

CHAPTER 1

Making Sense of Our Time—The Concept of Cultural Maturity

The future isn't what it used to be.

— Yogi Berra

THROUGHOUT MY PROFESSIONAL LIFE, I have worked both as a psychiatrist and as a futurist. As a futurist, I've developed conceptual tools that help people make sense of the times we live in and trained leaders for the critical tasks ahead. In this book, I will primarily wear my futurist hat. But my work doing psychotherapy and my thinking about cultural change have frequently overlapped in ways that have affected me deeply. One encounter often comes back to me when people ask me whether I think we should be hopeful when we look to the future.

Alex was fifteen when he came to me for counseling. As he sat before me in his jeans and sweatshirt, he looked like the average American kid. But two days before our conversation, Alex had strung up a rope in his attic and tried to kill himself.

After taking time to get to know him, I asked Alex why he had wanted to end his life. He looked away, then down at his hands. Finally he offered, almost distractedly, "Things aren't going that bad." Then, after a long pause, he spoke to me more directly. "It's not so much about me," he said. "It's about everything. When I look ahead—into the future—I only feel depressed. I just don't see a life I'd want to live."

Alex visited me regularly in the months following his suicide attempt. Sometimes his reflections were personal, but just as often they touched on larger concerns. I came to value our time together more and more. At one point he deftly turned the tables of the conversation.

"Tell me," he asked, "what do you think about the future? Do *you* think anything we do today really matters?"

In fact, I believe these are amazing times to be alive—not simple times, but amazing times nonetheless. Yet it can be hard to put just why into words. Of course, we see stunning technological advances and social issues well worth our creativity and commitment. But Alex's question went deeper. To know whether "anything we do today really matters" requires that we reflect deeply on who we are and what life in our time is about.

As I searched for just what to say, I thought about how the cultural stories we have most relied on in the past often fall short of what we need today. We have stories like the American Dream, with its focus on individuality and economic prosperity. We have the Industrial Age's promise of ever onward and upward technological advancement. We have our many and varied religious traditions. Each of these, in different ways and at different times, has served us well. But none of them—alone or even together—seem sufficient for the challenges we now face.

Today, new narratives are often put forward as alternatives. Some people assume that the transformations of the Information Age will assure a dramatic and vibrant future. Others are more pessimistic, believing that the profound environmental crises we face may be beyond our power to address. Some see, with the end of the Cold War, new hope for a peaceful and democratic world. Others, again less positive, see mostly aimlessness and the decay of traditional values and institutions. Still others offer even more extreme positive and negative interpretations. Maybe we are entering a spiritual New Age? Or instead, a time of moral downfall, of impending Armageddon?

But while these additional stories may reflect aspects of what lies in store, in the end they represent competing, partial worldviews rather than the comprehensive kind of understanding that our times require. This short book offers an overarching viewpoint. Think of it as a response to Alex's challenge to tell him about the future. *Hope and the Future* is written more for adults than for youth—significant life experience is needed for the ideas in this book to make solid sense. But Alex's concerns touch at the heart of it.

The Question of Hope

Should we be optimistic about the future? There are good reasons not to be. As a species, we face immense new challenges—from global terrorism, to climate change, to frightening economic uncertainties. And we humans often do very dumb and shortsighted things, particularly when faced with demanding and confusing circumstances. It is not at all clear that we are up to what our times ask of us.

I will argue here that hopefulness is warranted, at least if we can bring the needed courage and perspective to bear. And I will address what that courage and perspective must accomplish. I will describe the possibility—and necessity—of a critical next step in our human cultural development, of an essential "growing up" as a species.

I call that new developmental step *Cultural Maturity*. People tend to assume that Modern Age beliefs and institutions represent ideals and end points. The concept of Cultural Maturity proposes that our Modern Age worldview cannot be an end point, that further changes are necessary—and happening. Possibility is not destiny, and there are many ways in which we could hide from all that this needed growing up will require. But if the concept of Cultural Maturity is accurate, a positive future—indeed, a future of striking significance—becomes very much an option.

The concept of Cultural Maturity supports hope most immediately by making clear that a positive way forward exists. It provides a future narrative to replace what we have known—and a compelling one. If there is a single core crisis in our time, it is a crisis of purpose—in the end, a crisis of story. To make good choices in times ahead—and to continue to advance—we must have new ideas and images to guide us. Ultimately, we need a new defining story just so we will have the courage to continue. Without some way to see order in events that can often seem arbitrary or chaotic, we, like Alex, can lose hope.

The concept of Cultural Maturity also supports hope by providing practical guidance. It offers specific tools for taking on the tasks ahead. This book will examine the assertion that not only are more and more of the challenges we face as a species difficult to address, effectively addressing them will demand new human capacities—that we learn to think, act, and relate in some fundamentally new ways. The concept of Cultural Maturity helps us make sense of what these needed new capacities involve and what happens when we apply them. It also describes how, when we are ready for them, they can be learned and practiced.

In addition, the concept of Cultural Maturity supports hope by clarifying how the needed new ways of thinking and acting may be more readily realized than we might imagine. The developmental nature of a term like "maturity" points toward how, at least as potential, the needed new capacities are "built into" who we are. If this conclusion proves true, then the future becomes more about commitment and perseverance than about inventing new abilities from scratch. This book will look at both evidence for this conclusion and at ways in which we are already beginning to acquire the needed new capabilities in many parts of our lives.

Cultural Maturity is not as easy a notion as a simple phrase like "growing up" might suggest. At the very least, this is a specific kind of growing up, less about the fresh freedoms of adulthood than the greater sense of perspective and proportion that comes with life's later maturities.[1] And to understand it deeply, we must appreciate the changes in ourselves that underlie the new capacities it describes. But the concept of Cultural Maturity is accurately a single encompassing idea. And as with any notion whose time has come, when we are ready for it, it can seem like common sense. What is different is that this is a degree of common sense that before now we could not have fully grasped, nor really tolerated.

Culture in Evolution

The concept of Cultural Maturity is unusual because of the big-picture vantage it reflects. In contrast with future-oriented social commentary that stops with the next election cycle, business cycle, or news cycle, it is concerned not just with immediate issues, but with humanity's long-term well-being. Just as much, it is unusual because of

---

1 People use the word "maturity" to refer to two different points in personal developmental processes—the changes that take us from adolescence into adulthood, and those that come with taking on second-half-of-life developmental tasks. The concept of Cultural Maturity makes reference to the second kind of change process. We will examine how this distinction is key for the developmental analogy to be of value.

the developmental picture of change it draws on. While most people recognize that humanity has advanced over time, we tend not to appreciate the depths of the changes through which advancement has taken place. And certainly we tend not to appreciate the depths of the changes needed in our time.

In fact, a look to history supports the conclusion that all major historical hinge points reflect change of a generally developmental sort. Events around the globe in recent decades, most notably in the Middle East, illustrate this kind of change. We've seen dramatic shifts with the overthrow of long-entrenched authoritarian regimes and at least the beginnings of more democratic structures. Much of the excitement people feel with these changes comes from the recognition that these countries are witnessing the beginnings of a fresh chapter in culture's story (however messy these change processes can be).

I find it curious that even people who recognize that events such as those in the Middle East today involve a "next-chapter" sort of change tend not to apply this developmental way of thinking to modern realities. The kind of change that produces the emergence of democratic principles happened for people in the modern West well back in our history—in the U.S. with our original emancipation from colonial rule and the first forging of constitutional documents. The changes described by the concept of Cultural Maturity are similar to those we see in other parts of the world today in that they are also products of their times. But Cultural Maturity has to do with a further essential chapter in our human evolutionary story.

Understanding that new chapter is the task in these pages. We will examine how Modern Age belief is profoundly limited when it comes to addressing the important questions before us, and how if we hold to such belief as dogma, it undermines our going forward. We will also examine how Cultural Maturity's changes provide a new sophistication in our worldview that can both inspire in our time and offer concrete guidance for addressing the challenges ahead.

Most people today recognize—consciously or not—that something like what the concept of Cultural Maturity describes will be increasingly necessary. We understand that a sane and healthy future will require us to be more mature in our choices—or at least more intelligent. People see that the growing availability of weapons of mass destruction, particularly when combined with our ever more globally interconnected world, means that we must bring greater insight to how we relate to one another. And we appreciate that making good long-term choices in a world with limited energy resources will require a newly sophisticated engagement of hard realities. Our more immediate frustrations also frequently reflect an acknowledgement of the need for greater maturity. More and more often today, people feel disgust at the childishness of political discourse, and at how rarely the media appeal to anything beyond adolescent sensibilities.

Most of us also recognize something further. We see that it is essential, given the magnitude and the subtlety of the challenges we face and the potential consequences of our decisions, that our choices be not just intelligent, but wise. Cultural Maturity is about realizing the greater complexity and depth of understanding—we could say "wisdom"—that human concerns of every sort today demand of us.[2]

People today often express concern that we in the modern West might be in a time of decline. Certainly we are in a time of major change. The concept of Cultural Maturity proposes that there is no reason that the future needs to be one of decline or collapse—at least not if we respond to today's challenges with the necessary sophistication. What we see, ultimately, is the possibility of a new, more mature—even wise—kind of human identity and significance.

Cultural Maturity's Changes

Cultural Maturity involves two related change processes that are each today fundamentally reordering the human experience. The first change process concerns our relationship as individuals to culture as a whole; the second concerns basic changes in how we understand.

---

2 Some care needs to be taken if my use of the term "wisdom" is to be helpful. The kind of wisdom I refer to is different from wisdom in the idealized sense often found with romantic notions of the sagacity of elders, and also from specifically spiritual associations often seen with references to "perennial wisdom." It is of a more gritty sort. But framed in the way I will use it here, as a set of developmental imperatives, wisdom becomes quite specifically what Cultural Maturity is about.

We can see evidence for the first kind of change in an increasingly common recognition: Cultural absolutes—such as nationalistic notions of identity, clear moral codes, and socially defined gender roles—no longer provide the same reliable guidance that they once did. Part of this loss is a simple product of globalization. It is hard to hold to absolutist convictions when they so obviously collide with other people's completely different, yet just as absolute beliefs. But the concept of Cultural Maturity proposes that this challenging of past absolutes also has deeper, more developmental roots. Before now, culture has functioned like a parent to the lives of individuals. It has provided us with our rules to live by, along with our sense of connectedness, identity, and security. Cultural Maturity's societal "growing up" makes culture's parental function increasingly something of the past.

Today's questioning of traditional cultural assumptions is often given emphasis in postmodern writings, and it has inspiring aspects. Challenging old certainties offers new freedoms and reveals new options. But it can also affect us in disturbing ways. The weakening of traditional guideposts can leave us feeling overwhelmed and disoriented, set adrift in an increasingly complicated world. If we are to have real hope, we can't stop there. The questioning of traditional assumptions can thus be at best only a beginning.

The second kind of change that comes with Cultural Maturity provides an antidote to postmodern aimlessness. Cultural Maturity brings with it changes in ourselves—specific cognitive changes. These changes alter not just *what* we think, but *how* we think. In doing so, they make it possible for us to engage human purpose in deeper and more encompassing ways than in times past. As you will see, they also make possible the conceptual tools needed to address the future's increasingly complex and demanding challenges. Cultural Maturity's cognitive changes offer that we might again have guidance—not of the old cut-and-dried sort, but guidance that is ultimately more powerful.

We will examine how Cultural Maturity's changes stretch us in very basic ways—often in ways that can feel disturbing. But I will argue that we as a species really have no choice but to take on the challenge they present. We will look at how the most critical questions before us remain impossible to address—or fully make sense of—without the new skills and capacities that Cultural Maturity's changes make possible. We will also look at how we have made at least first-step progress toward realizing those new skills and capacities.

The Only Game In Town

I find a simple image helpful for representing the challenge that Cultural Maturity's changes today present. Think of a doorway marked by a threshold. (See Figure 1-1.) The other side of that doorway represents a territory of experience that is beyond us to fully understand when we are limited to familiar assumptions. Today we reside at an awkward in-between time with regard to Cultural Maturity's changes, straddling that threshold. These are not easy circumstances. But they are circumstances that make the times we live in and the choices that each of us now make particularly significant.

Fig. 1-1. Cultural Maturity's Threshold

Later, I will add detail to this image that makes it more specific to the changes that we confront in our time (the basic image could represent any change of a "next chapter" sort). I will also introduce a critical further recognition: Cultural Maturity's changes are of a particularly fundamental sort—both different from change processes we have seen in the past and of particular consequence. The general path that has gotten us to where we are through each of history's defining change points has, in an important sense, reached a dead end—there is really no way to continue forward as we have even if we wanted to.[3] Over the course of the book, we will examine how Cultural Maturity's changes address this seemingly dead-end circumstance. If what I describe is accurate, Cultural Maturity becomes, in effect, the only game in town.

Cultural Maturity is a specific concept within Creative Systems Theory, a comprehensive framework that helps us understand, among other things, how human systems grow and evolve. Within Creative Systems Theory, Cultural Maturity is a highly delineated and rigorously substantiated notion. It refers to a particular kind of maturational dynamic that happens at a predictable point in formative processes of all sorts. In this book, our interest with the concept of Cultural Maturity is more immediate and basic. I want to make clear—hopefully even inescapable—how it is that a next chapter in our human narrative has become essential. I also want to make clearly understandable how the concept of Cultural Maturity provides effective guidance for going forward.

The largest part of the book applies a "hands-on" approach. The next four chapters are organized around specific new capacities that we must acquire if we are to effectively address the challenges before us. These hands-on chapters examine what these new capacities involve, how Cultural Maturity's changes make them possible, and what it means to put them into practice.

Chapter Two looks at how going forward effectively will require stepping beyond the "us-versus-them" assumptions that have before been intrinsic to the experience of social identity. It examines how, if we can't leave such past tendencies behind us, stagnation—and devastation—becomes inevitable. It also looks at how we are beginning to take these needed steps. *do we change in order to avoid devastation and to who's benefit?*

---

3   See "The Rethinking Progress and the Dilemma of Trajectory" in Chapter Five.

Chapter Three explains how any hope of our making good future decisions hinges on a better appreciation of the fact of real limits. It looks at how we face essential constraints today both to what we can do and what we should do. It also looks at some of the surprising results we find when we relate to limits in more mature ways.

Chapter Four addresses how future success in human relationships of all sorts—from love to leadership—will require new ways of understanding what relationship itself is about. It also reflects on how changes in the ways we relate imply fundamental changes in who we are—changes in how we think about, and embody, human identity.

Chapter Five examines the need to revisit the truths we use in making our choices. We will look at how the future requires not just that we take greater responsibility in determining the truths we apply, but also that we conceive of truth in more nuanced and encompassing ways. One truth-related topic will get particular attention: the importance of revisiting our modern concept of progress—of asking afresh what it means to advance.

Each of these chapters reflects on some of the more provocative implications of the new capacity it addresses, and more generally, what that capacity can teach us about Cultural Maturity's changes. Each also examines how we can already see beginning steps toward realizing that new capacity in the best of contemporary thought and policy.

Chapter Six turns to understanding Cultural Maturity's changes more conceptually. Other books in this series address theoretical concerns in greater detail,[4] but these further reflections should provide a solid beginning sense both of the concept's theoretical underpinnings and the considerable evidence for its conclusions. We will more deeply examine how the developmental analogy that gives the concept its name—the parallel between second-half-of-life maturity in our individual lives and current changes in culture—helps us understand what Cultural Maturity's changes involve and what is unique about them. We will also briefly examine the cognitive reordering that produces these changes. And we will compare and contrast the kind of

---

4 See *Cultural Maturity: A Guidebook for the Future* or *Quick and Dirty Answers to the Biggest of Questions*.

perspective that produces the concept of Cultural Maturity with other ways of thinking about our human future.

Chapter Seven turns specifically to the question of hope. It looks back on the book's observations and expands upon each of the ways in which I've suggested that the concept of Cultural Maturity supports the appropriateness of hope—how it provides a compelling guiding narrative, how it makes needed new capacities understandable, and how it suggests that needed changes may come more readily than we might imagine.

The book's appendix provides a brief, frequently asked questions overview of the concept of Cultural Maturity. It addresses questions often asked by people who are not yet familiar with the idea. (Feel free to start there if you'd like.) It also provides a useful summary for people who have already started working with the notion.

Setting Training Wheels Aside

Some readers, at least initially, may find this book's conclusions disconcerting. Certainly, we face the fact that the kinds of changes I will be describing are new to us. And making sense of Cultural Maturity requires that we confront a chicken-and-egg conundrum intrinsic to developmental change: Any depth of understanding of the new capabilities we have interest in will itself require at least the beginnings of culturally mature perspective.

The way in which Cultural Maturity's changes are of a fundamentally different sort than change processes of times past can have especially disconcerting implications. Culturally mature perspective confronts sacred cows of all sorts—political, scientific, philosophical, religious, and more—and does so at the level of basic assumptions. It does not set out to do this; rather, the challenging of favorite beliefs is an inherent consequence of culturally mature perspective's new, more sophisticated vantage. But the fact that this result is benign doesn't necessarily make it comfortable.

It is not uncommon to hear people assert that somehow we need to grow up in our thinking, but most often what is being claimed is only that people should think more like us, agree with our particular ideological beliefs. The concept of Cultural Maturity presents a wholly different kind of challenge. It describes stepping beyond limiting ideological assumptions wherever we find them, and learning to think and act in new, more complete[5] and sophisticated ways.

I will draw on a couple of ways of thinking throughout the book that directly reflect this especially fundamental kind of challenge. Each will be essential to fully understanding Cultural Maturity and its implications. The first new way of thinking provides the most specific conceptual language for describing where Cultural Maturity's changes take us. I will describe how future understanding will need to be more expressly "systemic." At the least, it must do a better job of taking into account all that is involved, of better addressing the "whole ball of wax," whatever our concern might be. But I will propose that future understanding also needs to be systemic in a specific new sense. The kind of systems ideas needed to address the questions ahead must take us beyond the "engineering" sort of systemic thinking we've used to build bridges and great buildings. They must better address the fact that we are living beings. In the end, they must go further still and directly address the conscious and audaciously creative kind of life we are as human beings. The critical questions ahead are not just technical questions, nor even just "living systems" questions; they are, essentially and fundamentally, human questions.

The second new way of thinking gives us the evolutionary perspective that produces Cultural Maturity's implied developmental analogy. In some circles, the whole notion that cultures evolve is controversial—and often for good reason. Historically, thinking that sees societal change in evolutionary terms has been used to justify all kinds of misleading and dangerous conclusions. Chapter Six looks both at these legitimate objections and at how the developmental sort of evolutionary thinking that underlies the concept of Cultural Maturity avoids past traps. It also examines how Cultural Maturity's cognitive changes make this kind of thinking newly possible.

These significant demands acknowledged, by the book's conclusion, most readers should find the concept of Cultural Maturity surprisingly accessible. This accessibility will come partly from new insights, but it will be a product as much of the developmental nature of those

---

[5] When I use the word "complete," I do not at all mean finished. I mean complete in the sense of better including all the pertinent pieces.

insights. I've described how Cultural Maturity's changes, when timely, can feel like common sense. Victor Hugo famously observed that there is nothing more powerful than an idea whose time has come. When it comes to Cultural Maturity's changes, that time is now. Once we step over Cultural Maturity's threshold, it is the understandings of times past that then seem odd and complicated.

I think of the experience of effectively engaging Cultural Maturity's challenge as like that of a person who, in learning to ride a bicycle, at a certain point sets his or her training wheels aside. The riding task becomes more demanding, and initially the bicycle may feel less stable. But if the cyclist has done sufficient preparation and the time is right, setting training wheels aside need not be a problem. Indeed the result is inspiring. We discover a new, more complex and dynamic kind of stability—and much greater ultimate possibility. With Cultural Maturity, the potential result is similar.

An Introductory Exercise

When I lead workshops on the future, I often begin with a brief exercise. It makes a good starting point for this book's reflections. I strongly encourage you to take a moment with it:

■ *First, identify two or three challenges, concerns, or problems that you feel our species must at least begin to successfully address over the next ten to twenty-five years.*
Your choices could span from the most personal of concerns to the most global. All that matters is that each issue be something you care deeply about. You would feel personally troubled and pained if we failed to confront it successfully.

■ *Then ask yourself what will likely be needed to effectively engage each of these concerns. What skills, perspectives, policies, values, technologies, acts, or abilities will be required? Take time to reflect in depth.*
Be aware of your own thinking process as you explore options. Notice if you tend to be drawn most immediately

to particular kinds of solutions. For example, some people jump to more "external" answers: new laws, appropriations for social programs, or new technologies. Others are most drawn to answers of a more "internal" sort: deeper psychological awareness, a return to traditional values, or a "shift in consciousness." If one kind of solution alone isn't enough, be as specific as you can about what part of the task remains to be addressed. Let yourself be surprised by what you come up with. Often the awarenesses that turn out to be most important don't fit into ready categories, or they require that language be used in unusual ways. If the pieces don't immediately come together, try framing the question or problem in a different way. New challenges often require not just new answers, but also new ways of articulating the questions.

■ *Next ask yourself if any of the needed skills, perspectives, policies, values, technologies, acts, or abilities you listed are new. Which have always been part of being good citizens and leading healthy lives? Which require new sensibilities and capacities?*
Examine claims you make here very closely. Some people are overly quick to see the need for radical change. If you claim that some capacity is new, be very clear what makes it so. At the other extreme, many people share with Marcus Aurelius the assumption that there is "nothing new under the sun." If this is more your tendency, closely examine the terms and concepts you have used—responsibility, love, community, freedom, individuality, or morality, for example. Do these terms have the same meanings in the contexts you are using them as they did twenty, fifty, or a hundred years ago?

■ *Finally, notice any similarities between what your two or three challenges will require of us. Do common threads exist? If so, do these threads have any relationship to each other—do they in any way suggest a coherent fabric? And taken together, do they offer any useful information about the larger task of our time?*

The four chapters immediately ahead draw on issues and challenges people often choose in doing this stretching exercise. I've selected those I have to provide the most compact and stimulating introduction to the concept of Cultural Maturity.

CHAPTER 2

Addressing the Seeds of Conflict—
Toward an End to "Evil Empires"

War is the normal occupation of man.
— WINSTON CHURCHILL

A few questions:

1. Given the growing availability of weapons of mass destruction, how do
   we best guarantee a safe human future?
2. Is there an antidote to the petty partisanship that today so often
   undermines the effective functioning of government?
3. What is the purpose of ideology, and do useful ways of thinking lie
   beyond it?

Our exploration starts with one of today's most significant and
obviously needed new capacities: We must get beyond our historical need for enemies. This first capacity illustrates particularly well
how effectively addressing the challenges ahead will often require
fundamentally new human abilities. It also provides a provocative
illustration of how we are already making important progress.

Friends and Enemies

If Winston Churchill was correct that "war is the normal occupation of man," then the times ahead will not be bright. In
the not-too-far-off future, most nations will have ready access
to weapons of mass destruction—if not nuclear, then certainly
chemical or biological. And increasingly, such deadly capabil-

ity is becoming available not just to nations, but also to ethnic factions and terrorists. Like it or not, the weapons-of-mass-destruction genie is out of the bottle.

In making this claim, I do not mean to diminish the importance of efforts toward disarmament. I applaud anything we can do to limit, or at least slow down, the proliferation of deadly weaponry. But the simple fact is that unless we can somehow alter the tendencies that have made war such a central part of the human condition, hope for the future is really not justified.

The concept of Cultural Maturity suggests that our war-like tendencies are in fact alterable. To understand this possibility, we need first to examine the origins of human conflict. Competition for land and resources explains part of it. But the primary cause is more basic. Since our species' earliest beginnings, we humans have divided our worlds into "chosen people" and "evil others." We've viewed people like ourselves as in some way special, and projected the less pleasant parts of ourselves onto our neighbors.

If this "chosen people/evil other" dynamic is biologically hardwired, it is difficult to be optimistic. But as it turns out, this dynamic is just as much psychological as it is biological. Such polarizing has fulfilled important psychological needs. It has played a key role in establishing social identity and creating the close bonds needed for social order. More generally, by supporting absolutist belief, it has protected us from life's easily overwhelming uncertainties and complexities. But it is also the case that conflict has been a natural result. At least up until now, we've needed enemies—and we've made sure we've had them.

The recognition that psychological mechanisms come into play doesn't, by itself, provide a solution to the human conflict conundrum. Without a way to alter this historical inclination, we are no closer to an answer. But a more psychological picture does invite us to think about how further options might be possible. For example, it is reasonable to ask whether the global interconnectedness of today's world could provide a way beyond our past war-like tendencies.

Given the mechanism I have described, globalization may very well contribute to needed changes. As we come to better know people who are different from ourselves, we should find it easier to recognize what we have in common. But, unfortunately, globalization by itself can't provide the needed antidote. Greater proximity also has the potential to trigger conflict and inflame existing animosities. As Robert Frost reminded us, "Good fences make good neighbors."[1] This opposite kind of effect is something we already witness. I see the collision of cultures that before have had only limited contact as one of the major causal factors in modern-day international terrorism.

In the end, any hope for a peaceful future must come from a deeper kind of change. We must somehow see a lessening of the forces within ourselves that lead to war. If this is not possible, major conflict will be increasingly frequent, with historical tendencies toward violence, if anything, manifesting in ever more extreme ways. The world is becoming an ever more dangerous place to be someone else's "evil other." We must simply prepare as best we can.

A significant lessening of the psychological forces that lead to war might seem like wishful thinking. But the concept of Cultural Maturity proposes that not only is such change possible, the potential for it is built into our natures. The concept of Cultural Maturity describes how our past tendency to divide the world into "chosen people" and "evil others" is not intrinsic to who we are, but developmental—a necessary characteristic of culture's evolution to this point. It also describes how, at a certain time in our human story, leaving at least the worst of such tendencies behind us becomes a defining developmental task. The evidence is good that we humans are already making a start toward these changes.

Essential Progress

I think most immediately of the fall of the Berlin Wall. Few people anticipated it—and certainly not the suddenness of the wall's collapse. And while world leaders have taken credit for the wall's fall, I think

---

1 Frost, Robert, *Mending Wall: Poetry of Robert Frost*, Henry Holt and Co., 1969

political initiatives had at best a limited role in creating what we saw. More accurately, the absoluteness of belief and the knee-jerk polar animosities required to support the wall's existence stopped being sufficiently compelling. Put simply, people got bored with what the wall represented.

As important as the Berlin Wall's fall is what has happened—or not happened—since. With the end of the Cold War, "evil empire" animosities between the United States and the former Soviet Union transformed with unprecedented quickness, becoming a relationship of mutual, if often begrudging, respect. And in the modern world, we have not seen the past's adamant sort of polarization since the wall came down, this in spite of the fact that we have had ample opportunity to engage in such demagoguery.

The modern West's response to terrorism provides the most striking and significant further example—an example that will have only greater importance in decades to come. The 9/11 World Trade Center attacks brought conflict closer to home in the United States than at any time since the American Civil War. People could have easily made terrorism the new communism, a response that would have undermined any possibility of effectively addressing terrorism's threat. Or worse, we could have made the whole of the Islamic East the new "evil empire" and turned very real fears into a war between civilizations.

But while leaders in the West have sometimes played the demon card in response to terrorism, to a remarkable degree average citizens have not taken the bait. Most people today see terrorism as complex and dreadful, but not a product of people who are themselves evil.[2] Viewed from a historical vantage, this outcome is remarkable. With regard to the broader question of whether we are up to what Cultural Maturity's changes more generally require, it provides valuable encouragement.[3]

---

2 Creative Systems Theory sees terrorism to be an inevitable consequence of globalization pushing together cultures that reflect different cultural stages.

3 The fact that the modern West and the countries where terrorism tends to originate reflect different cultural stages adds to the challenge of avoiding knee-jerk demonizing in response to terrorism—and also adds to how remarkable it is that we have responded as well as we have. That

In recent decades, the world has had no shortage of "holy wars": in Bosnia, Kosovo, Somalia, Mali, and between religious factions in the Middle East, to name just a few. But these were regional conflicts born from old ethnic and tribal hatreds. When the global community did get involved, it was most often in efforts to restore peace or to establish more representative leadership. And while the second Iraq war reflected dangerously misguided decision-making on the part of leaders (the situation with the war in Afghanistan is less clear[4]), the American people maintained an admirable degree of perspective. At least in more modern parts of the world, it appears that polarized images of ally and enemy are simply becoming outdated.

If the concept of Cultural Maturity is accurate, people should find it increasingly obvious that the mechanisms that in times past have so often led to conflict no longer serve us. Certainly, such mechanisms no longer serve to make us physically safer—in a globally interconnected world, safety is dependent on everyone feeling safe. If we can't step beyond our past tendency to demonize on the world stage, Pogo's quip that "We have met the enemy and he is us" will become not just the truth, but quite possibly the end of us.[5] But it is also the case that such mechanisms more

---

a person might choose to be a suicide bomber can seem only crazy if we limit ourselves to the individualist worldview of Modern Age belief, as can making an "insulting" cartoon or movie a reasonable justification for wide-spread retaliation. We also face how efforts to reach across this cultural divide rarely have the effect we might hope—indeed, such efforts often only make matters worse. We can remain the "great Satan" in the terrorists' eyes even with the most mature of responses. (See *Cultural Maturity: A Guidebook for the Future* for a closer look at the dynamics of terrorism and what a culturally mature response to terrorism looks like.)

4   The war in Afghanistan was more justified, but the fact that Afghanistan reflects an even earlier cultural stage made success of a dramatic sort even less likely. See *Cultural Maturity: A Guidebook of the Future* for a look at the contrasting circumstances in Iraq and Afghanistan (including an examination of how the different cultural stages reflected by each country affected likely outcomes).

5   Kelly, Walt, *The Best of Pogo*, Simon and Schuster, 1982

and more often today fail to fulfill the more basic needs that they historically addressed. No longer do they provide the same clear sense of national identity and social cohesion, or the same reliable protection from uncertainty and complexity.

We appropriately give thanks that the consequences of such now-outmoded tendencies have not been much worse than they have been.[6] I suspect that the combination of ever more available and dangerous weaponry, globalization, and the rise of terrorism would by now have produced widespread devastation if we were not already making important beginning steps toward greater maturity on the world stage.[7]

Projection and Possibility

I've used the word "projection" in describing the psychological mechanism that creates us-versus-them polarization. Since projection is for some people not a familiar concept, let's take a moment to examine just how projection works. Understanding projection not only helps us make sense of past "chosen people/evil other" tendencies, it also helps us appreciate how new possibilities might be an option. When we project, we act as if elements in our own inner workings were in fact characteristics of people or groups outside of ourselves. We attribute systemic parts of ourselves that we are not yet ready to acknowledge to other systems.

The personal development analogy provides insight into the dynamics of projection. Projection is an unconscious mechanism we see with immature personal behavior all the time. When we say a person is being adolescent, reactive, or blowing something out

---

6   During the Cuban missile crisis, we came frighteningly close to what could have been nuclear catastrophe on a massive scale.

7   It is important to emphasize that a culturally mature relationship to conflict differs fundamentally from simplistic conclusions people often reach about world peace. Culturally mature global policy is not about siding with peace against war. Nations need good defenses and a willingness to fight courageously when necessary. Later we will look at how this sort of misperception illustrates a common kind of conceptual trap. (See "Creative Systems, Polarity, and Intelligence" in Chapter Six.)

of proportion, projection almost always plays a role. The person attributes to the world threats and possibilities that have more to do with himself or herself.

We are not as used to recognizing when projection happens at a cultural scale, and we are certainly not as good at catching it when it does. The simple fact that projection has been inextricably tied to culturally shared beliefs explains a lot of it—when everyone around us believes a certain projected truth, it becomes very difficult for us to hold a different view. But there are also reasons more specific to the nature of belief in times past. In Chapter Six, I will describe how Modern Age belief, like belief in all previous cultural stages, inherently lacks the kind of perspective needed for the most defining of cultural projections to be recognized.[8]

At this point in our inquiry, the important recognition is that projection very much plays a role in our collective behavior—and hugely affects our shared beliefs and behaviors. And there is one further critical recognition: If the concept of Cultural Maturity is correct, this circumstance need not be the end of the road. The concept of Cultural Maturity clarifies how success with reincorporating projections at a cultural scale is not just possible, but something we might expect.

The developmental analogy again provides useful perspective—in this case for understanding how getting beyond projection at a cultural scale might be an option. Reincorporating projections from our past is central to the mechanisms of second-half-of-life maturity in personal development. When we say someone is acting in a fully mature way, a more integrative picture—in which projection plays a minimal role—is much of what we are observing. Personal wisdom is about better getting our minds around the whole of whatever we are considering. This requires re-owning—reincorporating—our projections.

Throughout this book, I will describe how Cultural Maturity makes possible—and indeed is essentially defined by—related integrative mechanisms at a more encompassing scale. Recent successes with recognizing and reincorporating cultural projections such as those I

---

8 See "Cultural Maturity's Cognitive Reordering" in Chapter Six.

have noted are consistent with the conclusion that not only are we capable of getting beyond the dangers projection today presents, we may well be succeeding with this critical task.

Further Examples

With each of the examples I have presented so far, projection is accompanied by demonization and thus has a negative flavor. This is not always the case with projection. We often find systemic dynamics in which the idealized projecting of positive parts of ourselves plays the more prominent role. The whole notion that culture has functioned as a mythic parent to the lives of individuals reflects this more elevating and affirming kind of projective mechanism. And each of the specific examples I've noted has also included such positive projection; each has implied a complementary projective idealization of one's own kind—seeing those like oneself as in some way "chosen." In later chapters, we will examine other examples of idealized projection.

But with this chapter we will continue to give primary attention to projection's more demonizing manifestations. Besides us-versus-them dynamics between large social groups such as those we have just looked at, there are other more circumscribed ways in which such projective demonization has manifested in cultural systems. We encounter something similar, for example, with bigotry—such as racism, sexism, or discrimination on the basis of sexual orientation. Similar to what we see with conflict between nations and ethnicities, with bigotry, projection produces the denigration of those different from ourselves.

Bigotry provides a further important example in which we see progress with the reincorporating of cultural projections. At least in the modern industrialized world, bigotry has gradually become less of a defining social force. While we must not ignore how far we have yet to go, the election in the U.S. of a black president in our time is something truly remarkable. Just as remarkable is how quickly we have seen women rise to positions of major political and corporate leadership.[9] And few gay people I know would have predicted—

---

9 In the political world, think of Margaret Thatcher or Angela Merkel in

even just ten years ago—today's increasing level of acceptance of both gay marriage and gays in the military.[10]

Another place we commonly see projective demonization is in the political sphere—and here the situation seems to be getting worse, not better. Discourse in the halls of government, today, rarely comes close to the needed systemic maturity. Those who spend more time than I observing the daily workings of government affirm that while polarization and pettiness are nothing new, what we see today is extreme. Political analyst David Brooks put it this way in his *New York Times* column: "According to [the traditional] mentality, a big successful nation exists in a state of equilibrium between its many factions.... This ethos has dissolved, on left and right. The new mentality sees the country not as an equilibrium, but as a battlefield in which the people, who are pure and virtuous, do battle against the interests or the elites, who stand in the way of the people's happiness."[11]

The role of projection in partisan pettiness is worth a closer look both because of its importance to effective decision-making in our time, and because it illustrates how progress is not happening at the

---

Europe. In the United States, the 2008 election could have just as easily given us a woman president.

10 Fully appreciating how these changes relate to Cultural Maturity requires that we think about what getting beyond bigotry involves in more sophisticated ways than we are used to. In a similar sense to how getting beyond "evil empire" dynamics on the world stage is not about "siding" with peace, a culturally mature transcendence of bigotry is not the same as simply celebrating our commonality. One of the things culturally mature perspective does is help us to recognize—and find significance in—just how different from one another we can be. Equal rights, while of huge historical and legal importance, is best thought of as a culminating Modern Age achievement. A culturally mature transcendence of bigotry represents a further sort of accomplishment. It affirms the importance of equality, but just as much it results in a deeper appreciation for what makes each of us, as individuals and as social groups, particular. See "Relationship, Culturally Mature Identity, and the Modern Myth of the Individual" in Chapter Four for a closer look at how this works.

11 Brooks, David, *New York Times*, November 2010

same rate in all parts of our collective lives. In addition, it introduces the important recognition that Cultural Maturity's changes potentially alter not just the choices we make as individuals and social groups, but also the institutions in which we make them.

Culturally mature perspective doesn't dismiss strong partisanship. It highlights how polarized advocacy has, in times past, played an important role in driving effective political process.[12] And it very much celebrates difference and vigorous disagreement. But culturally mature perspective makes clear that at least the more simplistic and extreme of partisan advocacy cannot continue to serve us. The reason is straightforward: The most important challenges before us are systemic in nature. Partisan pettiness makes systemic perspective—and systemically conceived policies—extremely hard to achieve.

It is important to recognize that contrasting political views tend to be products less of reasoned reflection than they are of opposing, systemically partial assumptions about how things work. Take poverty: Are there people who can't put food on the table and who need the support of society to survive? Most definitely. Is it also the case that unhealthy dependencies can result if government automatically provides handouts? Certainly, this is also true. Take defense: Is it accurate that a nation must stand ready to defend itself and not hesitate to do so when needed? The answer is clearly yes. Is it also true that patience and diplomacy often provide the most effective defense? Yes, again. Take economics: Is it right to say that the competition of free markets supports prosperity and growth? Few lessons in the last century have been more transforming of societies. Is it also the case that economic competition without rules to keep excesses and corruption in check can result in great harm? Unquestionably.[13]

---

12 Creative Systems Theory describes how debate between extreme positions with the eventual seeking of compromise has been central to the mechanisms of Modern Age governance.

13 We find additional support for the conclusion that we are dealing with opposed, systemically partial perspectives in the passions that commonly accompany political position-taking. The intensity of sentiments makes clear that more than purely reasoned consideration is most often involved. And

In each of these examples, both polar statements have merit,[14] but either by itself lacks the needed systemic sophistication. And equally important for understanding what culturally mature decision-making requires of us, just seeking compromise gets us no closer to where we need to go. Splitting the difference between two distorted positions does not produce a systemic result. If our interest is systemically conceived solutions, falling off either side of the political roadway or walking the white line in the middle each leave us short and equally at risk—whatever the concern and whatever that concern's extreme positions.

It is not clear to me at this point how best to interpret the particularly extreme partisan pettiness we see today, especially in the United States. It is possible that this inability to relate to others' political views with even basic civility, much less with culturally mature perspective, is only a momentary annoyance rather than anything of great significance (a simple product, perhaps, of political cycles). Or what we see could have greater significance, but be transitory—a product of the magnitude of the challenges we now face rather than a reflection of something fundamentally amiss (human systems tend to polarize when they face challenges beyond what they can readily handle[15]). But it is also possible that the intractableness we witness is symptomatic of deeper change processes at work.

If the concept of Cultural Maturity is accurate, the implications of getting beyond polarized partisanship ultimately go beyond just helping us make government as we know it function effectively. As with our

---

the common stubbornness of differences provides good evidence that such irrationality involves projection. The fact that elections are commonly won by just a few percentage points provides further evidence. If we were not dealing with polarization and projection, the better candidate would more often be recognized and supported by a decisive margin.

14 This is not to suggest that the positions of the Left and Right always have equal merit. Indeed, sometimes neither side has much of substance to contribute. It is to observe, simply, that each polar statement reflects part of a larger systemic picture.

15 See the discussion of the concept of Capacitance in "'Creative Systems' Understanding" in Chapter Six.

time in culture more generally, we tend to think of Modern Age institutions as end points and ideals. Throughout the book, I will come back to the essential conclusion that further steps in the evolution of institutions of all sorts—including government—lie ahead. We will look at what a next chapter in how we think about government and governance might look like from multiple angles. But this need to get beyond projection and polarization and think more systemically is certainly one important piece. In today's particularly intractable partisanship, we may be seeing signs of government as we have known it simply ceasing to function.[16]

Whatever the most accurate interpretation of current circumstances, getting beyond partisan pettiness will ultimately be essential to the effective functioning of government. The important recognition at this point is that Cultural Maturity's changes support this result. Culturally mature perspective helps us step back and engage the often contradictory-seeming complexities of our concerns—hold tensions more generously and get our minds around the larger systemic processes they represent. When it comes to governmental decision-making, this will not necessarily result in greater agreement in debate. One of the defining characteristics of culturally mature perspective is that it increases our appreciation not just for how our ideas may relate, but also for how they may be authentically different.[17] Because of this, culturally mature perspective can result in greater real difference of opinion. But Cultural Maturity's changes do promise greater effectiveness of debate, and more creative results.

---

16 Later I will describe an important phenomenon common with the beginnings of transition into culturally mature territory. Often, along with new insight, we encounter thoughts and actions that are products of extending old realities past their timeliness that can seem simply ludicrous. Creative Systems Theory calls them Transitional Absurdities. (See "Going Too Far" in Chapter Five.) What we see in government today may best be understood as Transitional Absurdity.

17 See later in this chapter, "Relationship, Culturally Mature Identity, and the Modern Myth of the Individual" in Chapter Four, and "Creative Systems, Polarity, and Intelligence" in Chapter Six.

Do we see evidence of such change today? Certainly we find beginning recognition that things need to be different. Confidence in government today is embarrassingly and frighteningly low, and people commonly cite leaders' inability to work together as a reason for this lack of confidence. Increasingly, people recognize that our options may very well be either making solid progress toward working more cooperatively together or the dead-end conclusion that government is irretrievably broken and ultimately incapable of providing needed guidance.

Systemic Thinking and Culturally Mature Perspective

We should not expect insights that take us beyond projection and demonization to come easily. Part of the job of past worldviews has been to protect us from recognizing that these mechanisms, or the aspects of who we are that they hide, even exist. For projection to work, we must keep it out of sight and out of mind. But, consistent with Cultural Maturity's predictions, we more and more often today recognize these mechanisms and the roles they have played. And we are beginning to find ways to talk about them—and of particular importance, to talk about the benefits of getting beyond them.

I have drawn informally on the language of systems in these beginning reflections. The language of systems provides one of the most useful ways of thinking about what happens when we reincorporate projection. The result when we reincorporate projection is a more complete—and thus more "systemic"—holding of experience.

But while the basic notion provides a start, as I suggested in Chapter One, the kind of systemic perspective we need for times ahead requires thinking systemically in ways that are quite new. Understanding what is necessarily new at all fully will require Chapter Six's more theoretical reflections. But at the risk of getting ahead of ourselves, we should take a moment at this point for a brief look at the kind of systemic perspective needed to effectively address the challenges we increasingly face. At least a basic grasp of what is necessarily new will be essential if issue-specific observations in the chapters immediately ahead are to fully make sense—for example, observations about addressing climate change, confronting the health care delivery crisis, the future of love, the challenges of contemporary leadership, or rethinking progress. Understanding this result will also provide important support for the essential claim that Cultural Maturity's changes produce a fundamentally different kind of outcome than we've seen at any previous major change point.

The most common sorts of systems ideas have their roots in engineering models. They are systemic in that they recognize that wholes often equal more than the sum of their parts, and can often be very helpful. But as I suggested earlier, today's challenges almost always require more than they can provide. Today's important questions involve not just mechanical systems, but living systems, and more often than not, ourselves as living systems. We need systems ideas that are able to capture the fact that we are alive, and beyond this, that we are alive in the specific sense that makes us human. So that we might have a shorthand way to speak of this newly essential kind of understanding, here I will capitalize the term *Whole-System* to refer to it. In Chapter Six, we will examine how this more sophisticated kind of perspective is a natural product of Cultural Maturity's changes.

For now, a simple way of thinking about how systemic understanding becomes different with Cultural Maturity's changes helps point us in the right direction. It draws on the fact that polarity has always before played a key role in human understanding.[18] A defining characteristic of culturally mature thought is that it "bridges" the polar assumptions of times past. Culturally mature perspective creates new links and associations—and not just between things we've seen as different, but between things that before we've often treated as opposites—for example, between mind and body, masculine and feminine, and even science and religion.

---

18 Creative Systems Theory describes how we can understand the defining assumptions of each previous stage in culture's evolution in terms of specific kinds of polar juxtaposition—such as what we see with objective and subjective in Modern Age thought. Plato observed that "we are all like pieces of coins that children break in half for keepsakes." Creative Systems Theory adds that we break that coin in characteristically different ways with each stage in any human formative process. *The Creative Imperative* looks in depth at the historical evolution of polarity. *Quick and Dirty Answers to the Biggest of Questions* provides an introductory overview.

We can recognize this kind of "bridging" of traditional extremes with each of the us-versus-them challenges that we have just looked at. Getting beyond projection on the world stage involves a "bridging" of ally and enemy; getting beyond bigotry requires a "bridging" of self and other; and getting beyond partisan pettiness demands the "bridging" of political left and political right.

We must take some care with the term "bridging," as it can suggest outcomes different from the kind of understanding we have interest in.[19] For example, while "bridging" in this sense is very much about relatedness, it is explicitly not about some simple joining. "Bridging" in this sense increases our appreciation for difference as much as for interconnectedness—a defining characteristic of culturally mature understanding that I noted earlier. But when the notion is fully grasped, it provides a highly useful conceptual tool able both to guide us in addressing specific issues and to alert us when we may be vulnerable to traps in our thinking.[20]

Culturally mature perspective "bridges" traditional polar assumptions not only when it comes to relationships between specific groups or particular ideas, but also within understanding as a whole. One particular "bridging" comes with questioning and stepping beyond culture's past parental function and in effect defines Cultural Maturity. Today's changes link ourselves and our societal contexts in a way we have not seen before.

Besides helping us understand why we might see more specific bridgings, this most basic bridging also helps clarify what bridging in this specifically systemic sense involves. Cultural Maturity is not about culture's role disappearing. What it is about is a new and deeper recognition of how the individual and culture relate, how each informs the other. It is also about making our understanding of both being an individual and relating with others more dynamic and complete.

This most encompassing linkage holds within it a multitude of more local "bridgings." We find in them some of the most

---

19 This is the reason I put the term "bridging" in quotes.

20 For a discussion of polar traps, see "Creative Systems, Polarity, and Intelligence" in Chapter Six.

compelling evidence that Cultural Maturity's changes are already taking place. Nothing more characterized the past century's most defining conceptual advances than how often they linked previously unquestioned polar truths. We encounter this in most fields, not just those that specifically concern ourselves. Physics' new picture provocatively drew a circle around the realities of matter and energy, space and time, the object with its observer, and more. Evolutionary biology came to link humankind with the natural world. And the ideas of modern psychology, neurology, and sociology have provided an increasingly integrated picture of the workings of conscious with unconscious, thoughts with feelings, and self with society.[21]

It is important to emphasize that the "problem" polarity presents today is not an intrinsic difficulty. It concerns the inability of polarized thinking to generate truth and meaning *in our time*. In times past, polarity worked. The polar antagonisms of church and crown in the Middle Ages, for example, were tied intimately to that time's experience of meaning, as were later Modern Age conflicts between competing positivist and romantic worldviews. That said, the concept of Cultural Maturity makes clear that polarized thinking has today very much become a problem. This becomes particularly the case when doing so is accompanied by projection and demonizing. The concept of Cultural Maturity also helps us understand how the needed more systemic understanding is now becoming not just an option, but a defining capacity.[22]

Later, in Chapter Six, we will look closely at how Cultural Maturity's cognitive changes make more encompassing kinds of understanding

---

21 The needed new kind of systems thinking is most obviously necessary if we are to effectively understand human concerns. But, in the end, how we understand alters our understanding of everything—including the physical and the creaturely. When we become able to think systemically in more dynamic ways, we become better able to follow reality's twists and turns whenever more dynamic understanding might prove useful. (See "'Creative Systems' Understanding" in Chapter Six.)

22 My second book, *Necessary Wisdom*, is organized around this concept of "bridging."

possible. For now, the developmental analogy again provides helpful associations. F. Scott Fitzgerald proposed as a sign of a first-rate intelligence (we might say a "mature intelligence") the ability to hold two contradictory truths simultaneously in one's mind without going mad. Through the changes that come when we effectively engage second-half-of-life developmental tasks as individuals, in any situation we come to better hold that whole of experience. We become able both to more fully step back from and to more deeply engage our complex, often contradictory inner workings. In doing so, we also become more comfortable with the complexities of our daily lives. Culturally mature perspective involves something similar with regard to our broader humanness.

We are only now beginning to grasp the importance of getting beyond the polarized assumptions of times past and to appreciate the implications of doing so deeply. And certainly we have just begun the task of learning to think with the needed systemic sophistication in the various parts of our lives. The fact that polarities reflect larger systemic realities might seem obvious, but in spite of the important successes I have noted, more often than not, we still miss how this is so. We can assume that minds and bodies are wholly separate even though daily experience repeatedly proves otherwise. We can think of how men and women understand and behave as not just different, but opposite, even though we find greater psychological variation between individuals of the same gender than we find on average between genders. And of particular pertinence to this chapter's reflections, we still too often accept that a world of allies and "evil empires" is just how things are—even as one generation's most loathed enemy became the next generation's close collaborator. The concept of Cultural Maturity proposes that the reason we still too often miss the "obvious" fact that polarities reflect larger systemic realties is that getting our minds around a more systemic picture requires a maturity of perspective that we are only beginning to be ready for.

In Chapter One, I promised to fill out the doorway image so that it would better communicate the particular nature of Cultural Maturity's changes. The concept of "bridging" helps do so. We can think of the columns on either side of the doorway's threshold as representing polar opposites. (See Figure 2-1.) I've described how Cultural Maturity's task involves walking through that doorway. When we do so, we "bridge" polarities, and the needed more dynamic and complete kind of systemic understanding becomes an option.

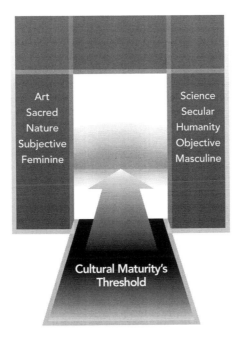

Fig. 2-1. "Bridging" and Cultural Maturity's Threshold

Besides providing a way to picture Cultural Maturity's task, the image also helps communicate how fundamentally different the result is when we succeed at that task compared to what we have seen before. Notice that this more detailed threshold image involves a bit of visual "trickery." The word "bridging" might seem to describe a pretty conventional result: joining the columns, what the doorway's overarching lintel might represent. But simply joining the columns would produce only adding, averaging, or oneness, depending on how we do the joining. As I've suggested, the outcome when we "bridge" polarities is not at all the same as adding or averaging—these at best produce compromise.[23] And

---

23 I've mentioned how middle-of-the-road political positions get us no closer to mature policy than the extremes of partisan advocacy.

certainly the outcome is different from simple oneness.[24]

The kind of action that produces "bridging" of the sort that results in culturally mature understanding—approaching the doorway's threshold, stepping over it, and making entry into the new territory beyond—has wholly different implications. This distinction is critical. When we confuse "bridging" with any of the previously mentioned things that it is not, we get misleading results. In the end, we get conclusions that undermine exactly what we wish to accomplish.[25]

A further simple image will have particular importance for our task in this book. It more explicitly depicts what we find on the other side of Cultural Maturity's threshold when it comes to human systems. Take a box of crayons. The crayons represent multiple systemic aspects. The box represents culturally mature perspective's ability to simultaneously hold those multiple aspects.

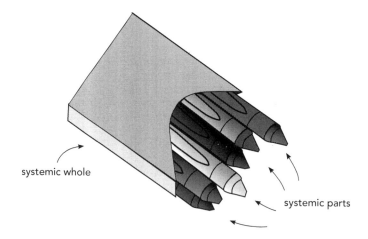

Fig. 2-2. "Whole-Box-of-Crayons" Systemic Understanding

---

24 A couple of earlier footnotes emphasized difference's essential contribution. I described how getting beyond "chosen people/evil other" dynamics on the world stage is not at all the same as "siding" with peace. I've also described how fully getting beyond bigotry is as much about more deeply understanding difference as it is about recognizing our commonality. Chapter Six addresses more conceptually why this is the expected result.

25 Later we will examine how a related kind of representational sleight of hand is needed whenever we wish to depict culturally mature outcomes. (See "The Dilemma of Representation" in Chapter Six.)

Later we will draw on this box-of-crayons image when exploring diversity of viewpoint. Once we get beyond polarization, we most often find multiple points of view. Recognizing a viewpoint's place within a more complex—multiple-crayon—systemic context can help us better understand both its practical utility and how it may fit—or not fit—with our own ideas, values, and temperament.

I will also use the box-of-crayons image to help clarify the changes in ourselves that produce Cultural Maturity. The image provides a simple yet remarkably accurate way to depict what becomes different with Cultural Maturity's cognitive changes. I will describe how culturally mature perspective allows us to both more fully step back from, and more deeply engage, our multihued, whole-box-of-crayons, human natures.

Complexity and Ideology

With this chapter, I have given primary attention to the importance of getting beyond our historical need for enemies and to the kind of systemic understanding needed to do so. But we could also talk about where these beginning reflections take us in a couple of related, more general ways.

First, we could think of reincorporating projections and thinking more systemically as being about more fully and deeply appreciating the richness of our human complexity. Before now, acknowledging human complexity in the ways increasingly required by today's questions would have been more than we could have tolerated. Cultural Maturity makes this more complete kind of engagement with our own—and the world's—complexities central to right thought and action. Culturally mature understanding is about engaging who we are—as individuals, in relationships, as societies, and ultimately as a species—with a complexity and systemic completeness of embrace that before now would have been too overwhelming to contemplate.

The related second way we can think about these beginning reflections contrasts this more complex, systemic result with the conclusions of ideology. Here I use the word "ideology" in a specific way—to refer to any belief that identifies with only one part of a larger systemic complexity. When we subscribe to ideology, at the very least we give that particular aspect of human complexity an idealized "chosen idea" status. Very often, we make it the whole of truth.

I've implied a couple of different ways in which ideology can manifest in our choices. Beliefs that identify with the assumptions of any one stage in culture's story are certainly ideological in this sense. For our inquiry, the recognition that Modern Age assumptions do not represent some last word—that future chapters in culture's story may yet lie ahead—has particular importance. Understood in this way, Modern Age belief as a whole becomes ideological.

We also confront ideological beliefs that exist at one particular point in cultural time—such as with political ideology. Commonly, ideological belief of this sort involves dividing a systemic whole into opposing half-truths and then projecting the half we find unacceptable. Ideology then reflects what the world looks like from the half of polarity that we claim. Ideology can also draw from a more complex array of systemic aspects. Ideology then becomes what we get when we take one "crayon" in our systemic box and make it final truth.

Cultural Maturity challenges us to step beyond ideologies of both the temporal, stage-in-development sort, and those that reflect here-and-now systemic differences. As we look to the future, we need to recognize that ideological views of both kinds fail to get us up to Cultural Maturity's threshold, much less over it. Postmodern perspective often gets us part of the way, but it too stops short. Postmodern thinking explicitly confronts ideology, but it rarely offers much of real significance to replace ideology's one-size-fits-all convictions.[26]

Cultural Maturity's changes explicitly take us beyond ideology. More than this, culturally mature perspective invites the possibility of nuanced post-ideological ideas, strategies, and ways of acting. Such changes in how we think and behave will be essential to effectively making our way. Later we will look at how the kind of developmental thinking on which this book is based reflects one

---

26 Indeed, because of postmodern theory's common aversion to overarching conception (and any real complexity of conception), postmodern thought often reduces to its own kind of particularly intractable ideology. French philosopher Jean-Francois Lyotard called this aversion an "incredulity toward meta-narratives." (See *Cultural Maturity: A Guidebook for the Future*.)

important expression of post-ideological understanding—under-standing that is systemic in a sense that effectively embraces our human complexity.

A quick summary:

Prior to now in culture's evolution, we have protected ourselves from life's uncertainties and complexities by dividing experience into simple either/ors and projecting aspects of who we are as systems onto systems around us. Thinking and acting in ways that more consciously reflect the whole of who we are is today becoming both increasingly necessary and more and more an option. Cultural Maturity makes possible post-ideological ways of understanding that better reflect the full richness and complexity of human experience.

The next chapter will examine a further way in which ideology has before served us, but now gets in our way. It has protected us from having to deal with the fact of real limits.

CHAPTER 3

Acknowledging Limits—
When Enough Is Enough

Once we accept our limits, we go beyond them.
— ALBERT EINSTEIN

A few questions:

1. How do we successfully address climate change and the very real possibility of environmental catastrophe?
2. How do we effectively confront our modern health care delivery crisis?
3. What is the ultimate significance of limits, and what does it mean to think in ways that honor them?

With our second needed new capacity, we turn our attention to the fact of real limits and the importance of more consciously acknowledging their presence. Recognizing real limits will be increasingly important to effectively addressing the challenges ahead. And appreciating the importance of doing so should play an increasingly central role in catalyzing the broader maturity of thought and action that the future demands. Recognizing today's necessary nos helps make tomorrow's new yeses both comprehensible and possible.

The Fact of Real Limits
Popular culture proclaims that if we only try hard enough, we can achieve anything—that ours is a time "without limits." Indeed, it suggests that we don't even have to try very hard. Ads for everything

imaginable tell us that we need only buy the right product and the miraculous will result. But while it is true that more is possible now than in times past, it is also true that consciously recognizing and maturely engaging limits has today become essential in a way it has never been before. Limits play a central role in almost all of today's critical challenges.

The most obviously important limits we face are environmental. We confront limits to energy resources, to clean air and water, to raw materials, to adequate food supplies, to habitat for the planet's species, and to space for the effluvium of civilization. The assumption that there is "more where that came from" applies less and less often. We also confront inescapable economic limits—limits to what we can afford. The increasingly common inability of governments to fund necessary services, along with the dangerously unsustainable levels of national debt that many countries maintain, provide striking evidence. In addition, we confront limits that are more specifically about us, such as limits to the usefulness of now-outmoded ways of understanding, and more generally to what we can ultimately know, predict, and control. These last sorts of limits directly inform all the others.

It is reasonable that we don't like to acknowledge limits. It is hard to imagine real limits doing anything but limiting us—making us less. It is also understandable that we might not be very adept at making sense of real limits and what they require of us. Not just our Modern Age narrative, but in an important sense the whole of the human story to this point has been heroic. When we've encountered limits, our task has been to break through them. And to a remarkable degree, we have succeeded at this task. In first becoming human, we stood upright, defying the limitations of gravity. Later we grew crops and built cities, confronting limits to growth inherent in our hunter-gatherer beginnings. In our time, we've sent people into space, transcending the very bounds of earthly existence.

But however grand such heroic achievements have been, more and more often today we confront limits that require a fundamentally different kind of response, limits that are inviolable. Neither the greatest of strength nor the subtlest of guile can take us beyond such real limits. Keeping inviolable limits at arm's length has become inconsistent with well-being, perhaps even survival. It is also less and less consistent with the experience of a purposeful existence.

The concept of Cultural Maturity describes how engaging limits in more mature ways represents a defining task of our time. It also helps us understand what effectively engaging inviolable limits entails. And it offers the possibility of thinking in new ways about limits and their implications.

Culturally mature perspective highlights how real limits are intrinsic to how systems of the sort we have interest in work, and also how acknowledging real limits can lead to the recognition of options—often profound options—that before now we could not see. With Cultural Maturity's changes, limits are no longer seen as the enemy of hope; instead they become intrinsic to any meaningful picture of hope.

Later in the chapter, I will describe how both the developmental analogy and the possibility of more systemic ways of understanding each support this more affirming picture of the significance of limits. But first let's touch on a couple of critical challenges—climate change and the health care delivery debate—where limits come into play. With both of these challenges, most people recognize that problems exist; these are front-page-news concerns. But we tend to miss the full nature and implications of the limits involved. And certainly we have a hard time getting our minds around how these challenges might be successfully addressed. With each, we'll look at how culturally mature perspective alters our relationship to limits and, in the process, makes effective solutions more possible.

Climate Change

Climate change presents our time's most publicized limits-related controversy. The question as it is commonly debated: Is human activity altering levels of greenhouse gases in the atmosphere to the extent that dangerous changes in the earth's temperature will be the result?

Arguably, the basic fact of climate change is not really a question anymore. The evidence is close to indisputable that significant global warming is already happening, and that it is of our making. Yet even though most people acknowledge that climate change is a major concern, we have made remarkably little progress toward addressing it. Why is this so? In part it is because the consequences of ignoring climate change are not immediate—it is future generations who will suffer most. It is also because of the magnitude of the potential consequences.

Contemplating them can overwhelm us. But I think it is also because, as a species, we have not before been capable of the needed maturity of perspective when it comes to the fact of real limits.

Because Cultural Maturity's changes make us more able to acknowledge real limits, they should significantly alter how we relate to the climate change challenge. They should help us better look squarely at the evidence. They should also help us more effectively evaluate steps we can take to minimize global warming's effects. And they should help us better anticipate consequences that we can't avoid and respond to those consequences in the most helpful ways. These contributions will be essential if climate change is not to essentially define the century to come. If global climate change is real, it has the potential to set in motion a truly apocalyptic cascade of events.[1]

For this chapter's look at limits, climate change most obviously confronts us with critical environmental limits. It challenges us to recognize that there are things we simply cannot continue to do. In the process, it also highlights limits to ideological beliefs that get in the way of thinking with the needed sophistication. The way culturally mature perspective helps us better evaluate risk provides insight. When we step beyond ideology, we become better able to weigh factors and determine their implications. This recognition applies to ideological assumptions of all sorts, both those of climate change deniers and those who are most ready to accept the global warming argument.

Effective risk assessment most directly challenges those who might simply dismiss climate change. How it does involves not just specific risks, but also how the climate change debate as a whole is framed. In

---

1 Current estimates suggest that even with the best of policies, greenhouse gas emissions could double by 2050. By the end of the century, that rate of change would produce temperature changes of between two and eleven degrees Celsius and sea level rises of between two and seven meters. Besides increases in weather-related disturbances such as hurricanes and cyclones, we would also be faced with dramatic flooding in low-lying areas, crop devastation with the increasing prevalence of famine, and growing economic instability. All of these effects have the potential to compound concerns we touched on in the previous chapter. For example, even if we see major progress toward Cultural Maturity, it will be hard to avoid significant exacerbation of human conflict.

proposing that the climate change question has already been largely answered, I was not claiming that we know for sure just what is happening and certainly not what the future ultimately holds in store. The best of science always leaves room for doubt. (It accepts limits to what is possible for us to know for sure.) But mature systemic perspective makes clear that recognizing the need for serious concern does not require us to be certain. All it requires is a basic willingness to look directly at the risks involved.

When I meet people who use the observation that we can't know for certain whether global warming is real to justify not responding to the climate change threat, I will often first agree that we can't know for sure, and then ask a couple of simple questions. I ask them what they think the odds are that, in fact, human-caused climate change is real. (I make them commit to a number.) I then ask them how they feel about their children playing Russian roulette. Few people are willing to claim that the odds of global warming being real and significant are less than Russian roulette's one in six. And those who claim that the odds are less than this have a very hard time escaping the conclusion that their beliefs have more to do with ideology than reasoned evaluation.

Ways in which effectively addressing risk challenges common beliefs of people who are more likely to immediately accept that global warming is real are most pertinent to the question of how we best respond to the threat. The "obvious" solution to climate change might seem to be to cut back on the use of fossil fuels in every way possible, as quickly as possible, and to replace them with renewable energy resources such as solar and wind power. But it appears unlikely that the more acceptable of renewable resources will be able to fill in the gap any time soon. And ultimately unhelpful approaches—or good approaches applied too rapidly—could easily harm more than they help. If we act inappropriately, we could see major economic upheaval. Widespread economic collapse could cause as much human anguish and damage to ecosystems as climate change, at least over the short haul.

The possible role of nuclear power in needed solutions provides a good place to see where more liberal ideology can interfere with effective risk assessment. A growing number of people who in the past unquestioningly opposed nuclear power are reevaluating it as perhaps necessary to any workable climate change strategy.[2] The suggestion can produce knee-jerk animosity. I have not made up my mind with regard to nuclear power's role. But I do know that effectively addressing climate change will require a willingness on everyone's part to reexamine views that are based on ideological assumptions.

Few challenges today present more complex dilemmas than climate change. If human-caused global warming proves to be real and as consequential it appears it may be, it will teach us about limits in no uncertain terms. Major portions of the damage are likely already beyond us to remedy. We can only hope that as much of the needed additional learning as possible can take the form of foresight and manifest as increasingly intelligent—perhaps even wise—action.

Culturally mature systemic perspective can't tell us exactly what we should do, or just what will happen even with the best of policy. But it does make clear that denial is not an option. It also makes clear that we must stay cognizant of as much of the systemic complexity involved as possible. This includes atmospheric and energy policy complexities, certainly, but it also includes all the various partial worldviews we might bring to making sense of climatic change and teasing apart future options. Avoiding widespread catastrophe will require newly mature— all-the-crayons-in-the-box—systemic perspective. It is hard to imagine how we will garner the needed nuanced and courageous response in the face of real limits without it.

Health Care—And Life's Ultimate Limit

The health care delivery debate provides one of the best demonstrations of the need to more directly acknowledge limits than we humans have been capable of to this point. The need to rein in health care costs is obviously about economic limits. But it also confronts us with more basic kinds of limits. It reveals limits to our modern heroic mythology. Ultimately, it brings us face to face with the most fundamental of human limits—our mortality. For me as a physician, it touches particularly close to home.

---

2 For example, Stewart Brand, one of the early leaders of the environmental movement, reaches this conclusion in his book *Whole Earth Discipline*. (See Brand, Stewart, *Whole Earth Discipline*, New York, Viking, 2009.)

Only a few years ago, the cost of health care was a topic of interest primarily to health care bean-counters. It is now broadly acknowledged that if we can't bring spiraling health care costs under control, health care expenditures, more than any other aspect of public spending, threaten to undermine the basic soundness of economies.[3] We tend to think of the health care delivery crisis as a battle between approaches—such as single-payer versus free-market—and to evaluate potential approaches by comparing them with solutions used in other countries. But the fact of the matter is that no kind of approach, however and wherever it is applied, will work unless we are willing to more deeply and fundamentally confront limits.

To understand just what reining in escalating costs will require, we must first recognize their source. The excesses of drug companies, doctors, hospitals, and the insurance industry have certainly played roles in rising costs. But the major cause is more basic—and not really anyone's fault. Today's spiraling costs are primarily a product of modern medicine's great success. Early innovations—like sterile technique and penicillin—were relatively cheap. More recent advances—sophisticated diagnostic procedures, exotic new medications, transplant surgeries, and more—are increasingly expensive and promise only to get more so.

It logically follows that containing costs will require more than the approaches commonly advocated. Current efforts at cost containment emphasize eliminating inefficiencies, getting rid of unnecessary procedures, addressing perverse incentives that reward quantity rather than quality of care, and better use of medical records. These are all very good things. But given the ultimate source of spiraling costs, none of these can be enough, alone or together.

The health care delivery crisis confronts us with a limits-related challenge that few people are ready to acknowledge, much less take on. Unless we are willing to spend an ever-expanding percentage of national resources on medical care, we have no choice but to limit the availability of treatment. Initially that means cutting back on procedures with no proven benefit. But eventually, too, we must be willing to restrict care that may be of benefit, but that is simply too

---

3 In the U.S., if the rising costs of Medicare and Medicaid are not addressed, getting the national debt under control becomes effectively impossible.

expensive. That means confronting the dreaded "r" word—I'll say it: rationing. We have to restrict medical services. To deny this fact is to waste our time debating policies that ultimately cannot work.

It might seem strange that we could miss such an obvious necessity—a high school student could do the math—but in fact it is not strange at all. Rationing care, by involving the conscious choice to limit treatment, presents a kind of human challenge we have not faced before. We've indirectly rationed care in the U.S. by making it difficult for people who can't afford care to get it, but that is not at all the same. Not providing care when we have effective care to offer calls into question modern medicine's heroic mythology. Modern medicine's task has been to defeat disease—essentially at any cost.

And that is the least of it. Rationing care demands a new relationship with death—life's ultimate limit. Medicine has always been about life-and-death decisions. But limiting care requires, in effect, the conscious choosing of death. Withholding care that might delay death's arrival is different only in name. Limiting care demands a maturity in our relationship with death that was not before necessary—nor, I would argue, within our human capacity to handle.[4]

I have met few people—and particularly in the political sphere—who recognize the full implications of the health care delivery crisis. In the current health care debate, neither the political left nor the political right has provided the necessary leadership. The Left claims that what it endorses won't result in the limiting of care—and unfortunately they are correct. The Right uses the word "rationing" as a condemning epithet. Both positions not only leave us short of useful answers, they ignore the hard and necessary questions. Effectively addressing the health care delivery crisis will make the controversies around more limited death-related issues such as abortion, assisted suicide, and capital punishment look like child's play.

---

4 A key function of traditional cultural narratives has been to shield us from the full meaning of death. Religion teaches that death is about entry into a more peaceful world (if we have not gone badly astray). Mechanistic science proposes that death simply returns us to the lifeless world of the inanimate (a final answer, if not a terribly inspiring one). Each view, in its own way, protects us from the magnitude of existential uncertainty and self-confrontation that a mature engagement with death ultimately requires.

A basic disconnect today pervades our thinking about health care and health care policy. We are beginning to recognize the economic train wreck that will result from not dealing with runaway costs. But at the same time, the media greets each new, ever more expensive medical advance with unquestioning fanfare. Somehow we have two stories that live in separate worlds. It is essential that we bring them together as two parts of a newly demanding—but now maturely systemic—picture.

I've mentioned how acknowledging limits can reveal options that were not before there to see. The health care delivery crisis provides a striking example of how this can be the case. Maturely engaging health care limits should contribute to increasingly powerful insights, and not just with regard to health care access. It should help us think in new ways about what being healthy involves, what health care should accomplish, and more broadly, the requirements of a healthy society.

In trainings, I've often done an exercise that engages people in the kind of decision-making that maturely engaging health care limits will require. I give participants a budget plus an envelope with patient profiles. People have to decide how that budget will be spent. Necessary decisions are invariably wrenching, but making them also always proves enlightening. Besides clarifying the kinds of choices we must learn to make, the exercise inevitably stimulates larger conversations about how we should spend limited resources. The group may want to talk about what it would mean to have a health care system that focuses as much on keeping people well as on fighting disease. Or it might want to examine how we should best think about the relationship between personal health and environmental health, or between personal health and the health of our communities.

In the end, acknowledging economic health care limits leads to rethinking health care fundamentally. Doing so increases demands all the way around, but it ultimately means that we do a better job of asking the right questions. It also means the possibility of a more whole-box-of-crayons systemic picture of both health and health care delivery. For today, isn't that just what the doctor ordered—a fresh, really big-picture look at the whole health care endeavor?

Limits and Individual Development

Effectively confronting inviolable limits such as those we've begun to look at in this chapter requires that we take on questions that are not just harder than we have before recognized, but harder than we have been capable of recognizing up to this point in our development as a species. It is important to understand how this needed greater maturity in the face of real limits might be an option.

Drawing on the analogy with personal development again provides insight. Understanding how our relationship to real limits changes over the course of a lifetime supports the conclusion that engaging real limits is possible, that limits don't need to represent some end of the road. It also helps make understandable what engaging limits maturely entails. And it helps clarify where effectively confronting real limits takes us—in particular, how doing so ultimately adds to our lives.

Learning to deal with limits in a grown-up way is another defining task of second-half-of-life maturity. An individual life's first half—like culture's story to this point—is appropriately heroic. Our job then is to dream, and when we face obstacles, to overcome them. Life's second half is always as much about appreciating the power of limits. This new relationship to limits comes close to defining maturity. When we successfully take on second-half-of-life developmental tasks, we come to see how, in real life, limits to what is possible come with the territory.

No fact better captures the developmental tasks of life's second half than limits that cannot be defeated in any familiar sense. With midlife, and the second half of life more generally, we face new physical limits—to our strength and agility, to how young and beautiful we can appear. We also face how certain of our dreams, often dreams closely tied to our sense of identity, may need to be set aside, or at least tempered. And life places before us, with an immediacy that would have been incomprehensible prior to this time, the fact of our mortality.[5]

As we confront this sudden barrage of new personal-life limits, we can at first seem to be at an impasse. If we stick only to how we have previously thought about things, we lack good options. When we deny these limits, our lives become increasingly absurd—thin caricatures of youth. Yet the opposite—to give up life's good fight—is only to become defeated and cynical. In fact, a way forward does very much exist, but

---

5 We have certainly before reflected on death, but midlife is the time when we first really "get it," the time when we first fully grasp our own death's inescapability.

getting there requires thinking and acting in new ways. More specifically, it requires that we think about and relate to limits in new ways.

The inescapable limits that become apparent with personal maturity at first can feel not at all welcome (and many never do). But if we can meet them creatively, they add to who we are. At the least, limits we necessarily face in the second half of life have important lessons to teach. Confronting limits to our physical strength teaches us about more subtle, and ultimately more important, kinds of strength. Confronting limits to youthful beauty reveals to us more enduring kinds of beauty. Confronting what may not be possible reminds us what is essential. And confronting our mortality—if we really do it—adds to who we are in an especially defining way. [6]

We don't have good words for where maturely engaging limits in individual development ultimately takes us—toward an expanded sense of proportion and perspective, a new humility, a fresh appreciation for contradiction, a deepened connection with the unfathomable. The word "wisdom"—used in the specific sense I've proposed—perhaps best captures the task of life's second half. Limits represent wisdom's ultimate teacher.

Confronting real limits requires wisdom, and at the same time makes us more wise in the process. And death, being life's final limit, presents these lessons with particular directness. When we engage the inescapable, and do so incorruptibly, our lives become newly vivid and robust—for no other reason than that human life *is* these things.

All of this is not to ignore the fact that the limits intrinsic to life's second half can present particularly demanding challenges, or to deny that such limits can result in as much pain as possibility. My point is only that personal maturity's picture is consistent with the recognition that limits can have an important—indeed generative—role in the life of human systems. The fact that the second half of life, well-lived, is as much or more about growth as the first at least supports the assertion that limits need not diminish us. And the fact that a new maturity in

---

6 Ask yourself a simple question: When you get to the Pearly Gates—or whatever you suppose we get to—what will you most want to be able to say about your brief time on the planet? No other question more quickly puts life in perspective.

our relationship to limits directly contributes to this growth supports the more striking conclusion that engaging real limits can result in new possibility. As important is the implication that the capacities needed to engage limits maturely are not foreign to us. At least as potential, they come part and parcel with being human.[7]

Engaging Limits

If we are to effectively address questions that involve real limits, it helps to have a sense of the process we go through in maturely engaging limits. Successfully grappling with limits tends to involve a predictable series of experiences. Not surprisingly, this sequence follows the steps we often go through in grieving an important loss. Acknowledging limits always in some way involves the death of a once-cherished heroic dream.[8]

First comes denial. We keep the limit—or at least the recognition that addressing it will require anything new—at arm's length. Second comes begrudging acknowledgement. Initially when we recognize a limit, we tend to feel disturbed by what we encounter. Third comes more overt acceptance. We grasp more fully how that limit is intrinsic to how things work. Finally, we begin to recognize how that limit, if engaged maturely, offers options we have not before recognized.

Limits to environmental resources make a good example. Until recently, most people kept the challenges presented by the natural

---

7 One could take issue with how I've applied the developmental analogy with limits. The reason we see limits with the second half of human development could be simply that individual human beings necessarily age and die—something not inherent to cultural systems. Creative Systems Theory describes how the analogy holds by virtue of dynamics that accompany the second half of any kind of human formative process. See Chapter Six, and for greater detail, *Cultural Maturity: A Guidebook for the Future*.

8 To be more complete, we should say "heroic/romantic." Modern Age stories reflect either heroic or romantic narratives (or both at once). Each kind of narrative in its own way denies limits, the first by assuming that limits can be defeated, the second by dissolving limits in magical connectedness. Chapter Four introduces this second kind of narrative. Chapter Six clarifies what each kind of narrative involves and how each has contributed to Modern Age thought.

world's limits far out of sight and mind—in spite of ample evidence that such limits are inescapable. Even if people acknowledged the existence of limits to resources, they assumed that future technical advances would make the perceived limits irrelevant.

Today, we tend most often to reside in the second, begrudging acknowledgment stage. We recognize such limits, but we relate to them primarily as realities that diminish us. Such basic acknowledgment represents a start, but ultimately only that. If we see the task only as learning to do with less, we remain well short of a solution. Most people find "doing with less" unconvincing as an ultimate solution— and appropriately so. Because of this, even when warnings about environmental limits are heard, too often they are not heeded.

Further understandings are needed—ones we are starting to appreciate. At the least, we need the further insight offered by the third step I've mentioned. We must recognize that environmental limits are not problems as much as they are inescapable aspects of how healthy systems work. In the end, we also need at least a bit of the final step. We need to recognize how respecting environmental limits enhances the purpose and potency of our human experience. This last step fundamentally alters the conversation and reveals choices that we might not have considered before.

It begins with the recognition that thinking of resource limitations in terms of "doing with less" captures only part of the picture. We must also understand "more" in fuller ways. Clearly, the mature acknowledgment of limits makes for a healthier planet, and that benefits everyone. But recognizing the importance of resource sustainability[9] also leads us toward questions at the heart of our modern crisis of purpose, questions about the nature of abundance (about when enough is enough). Considering such questions provides a critical antidote to times in which what often most defines us—and links us—is how much we consume. The result is a new and deeper, ultimately redefining appreciation for the diversity of factors that make a human life rich.

We see this same progression manifest more broadly with the weakening of cultural absolutes that comes with Cultural Maturity's

---

9 Fulfilling one's needs without diminishing the options of future generations.

changes. Today's loss of familiar guideposts does not make life easier. Initially, we may fall back on denial. But with time, we realize that the loss of former absolutes is in fact the loss of a surety that never really was—the death of once-necessary illusions. This may at first evoke only fear or despair. But as we step over Cultural Maturity's threshold, we see that what these changes ultimately mark is the possibility of more nuanced and complete truths—ways of understanding that better reflect the full richness of being human.

Limits and Culturally Mature Systemic Understanding

All these reflections tie directly to the importance of thinking more systemically—and thinking systemically in the new, more dynamic and complete, Whole-System ways I have described. Systemic perspective helps us better appreciate the fact of real limits. Even the most basic kinds of systemic understanding help us recognize how some things are appropriately not possible and also how, even when something is possible, what we *can* do and what we *should* do may not be the same things. Culturally mature perspective, and the more encompassing kind of systemic understanding it makes possible, provides particular insight into what it means to engage limits with the needed sophistication, and also into how doing so can reveal options that before were not possible to recognize.

A simple recognition makes the connection: Limits come with the territory with the kinds of systems we have interest in. Limits aren't just inconvenient obstacles that now and then raise their ugly heads. This is the case with most any kind of systemic reality. But certainly with the kind of systemic complexity we manifest by virtue of being human, limits come part of parcel with how things work.

The two primary examples I've used in this chapter illustrate this inherent relationship. With neither climate change nor the health care delivery crisis is the task to deal with some ultimately surprising circumstance. Rather it is to acknowledge the inescapable. Addressing climate change requires that we confront hard realities—and at a whole new level. But, in the end, what is being required of us is only that we recognize the natural consequences of our actions. And while we may at first miss that spiraling health care costs leave us no choice but to engage death more maturely, this observation is not ultimately complicated or obscure. Step back and think about health care limits systemically, and the conclusion becomes rather obvious.

Appreciating that real limits are intrinsic to how systemic processes work helps us see how real limits need not be the end of things. It also makes more understandable how engaging real limits might reveal new possibilities. In the end, engaging ultimate constraints teaches us about thinking in more systemically complete ways, and with that comes the recognition of new options. I am brought back to Einstein's perhaps paradoxical-seeming words at the chapter's beginning: "Once we accept our limits, we go beyond them." When we more fully take in all that is involved in any particular challenge—including real limits— we also better see what is ultimately possible.

Recognizing how limits and systems relate also provides additional insight with regard to ideology and how our relationship to ideology changes with culturally mature perspective. I've described how ideology protects us by taking one aspect of a larger systemic complexity and making it the whole of truth. Ideology also protects us by hiding from us the fact of real limits. It is in the nature of ideology that it makes claims for limitlessness.

We see this protective, limits-denying function most readily in ways of thinking that continue to reflect culture's past mythologized, "parental" status. Whether framed in terms of my-country-right-or-wrong nationalism, narrow religious belief, or thinking that makes science and technology gospel, such views imply an ultimate—and thus ultimately limitless—seat of truth. Parentally conceived truths are, in the end, omniscient and omnipotent truths.

Limitlessness is similarly implied whenever polarity reigns. Polar truths stop short of the needed maturity of perspective if for no other reason than that they are half-truths. More specifically with regard to limits, they stop short because their stories argue for limitlessness. We hear limitlessness proclaimed with polarities of every sort—political left versus political right, masculine versus feminine, leader versus follower, mind versus body, material versus spiritual, or good versus evil. Sometimes the source of the perceived limitlessness is a belief that the pole opposite to whatever we identify with is an enemy to be defeated. Succeed and all will be eternally well. Good defeats evil and we enter the kingdom of heaven. Political left defeats political right—or the reverse—and ideological purity conquers all. In other instances, the source is precisely the opposite. Instead of projecting our demons, we project images of ultimate truth. In the chapter to come, we will look at how this dynamic plays out with love and with leadership. When we put lovers and leaders on pedestals, we imagine that they have the power to make us ultimately fulfilled.

The recognition that Cultural Maturity brings with it the "bridging" of polarities helps solidify the relationship between limits, ideology, and culturally mature systemic understanding. It also further clarifies how engaging real limits can produce new possibilities. When we "bridge" any polarity, we "bridge" not just opposing systemic positions, but two opposing claims for limitlessness. The more systemic picture that results reveals such claims, however reassuring they might once have been, to be groundless. The new picture lacks the certainties and ready heroic excitements that the old polar realities provided, but, in the end, it invites a more dynamic and complete—and possibility-filled—kind of understanding.

The box-of-crayons image provides a more multifaceted way of thinking about the relationship of limits, ideology, and new possibility. Any "crayon" in isolation—say, one stakeholder in a complex negotiation or an expert in one particular field—may claim limitless significance for its particular vantage. With whole-box-of-crayons understanding, we recognize the illusionary nature of any single-crayon perspective's claim. In the process, we become better able to appreciate a question's complexities, and, as a result, we make more intelligent choices. And because whole-box-of-crayons systemic perspective makes it possible to address complexities of the particular sort we find with human life, often we can recognize options that are not just more intelligent, but in potential, more wise.

Along with helping us appreciate what a mature relationship with limits entails and makes possible, recognizing how limits, ideology, and systemic understanding relate also helps us avoid having our efforts ambushed by ideology. The health care example illustrates this. You've seen how the primary cause of the health care delivery crisis is ever more expensive treatments. But expensive procedures would not be a problem were it not for ideology. I've described how modern medicine's heroic mythology makes defeating death and disease—essentially at whatever the cost—health care's ultimate calling. To find useful solutions, we need to understand how ideological belief has contributed to the health care crisis. We also need to develop more systemically encompassing ways to think about health care's purpose.

Recognizing how limits, ideology, and culturally mature systemic understanding relate helps us in other ways by highlighting some of the broader implications of maturely engaging limits. For example, it helps us understand the ultimate reward for doing so: Acknowledging real limits opens the door not just to specific new possibilities, but also to culturally mature systemic understanding more generally. There is also how it confirms that the "solution" when we encounter inviolable limits of any sort is ultimately the same. The answer lies with culturally mature perspective and the greater capacity to hold life large that it makes possible. Beyond Cultural Maturity's threshold, it is our old ways of thinking—with their implied dreams of limitlessness—that become limiting.

Progress with Limits

The climate change and health care examples involve limits-related issues where we have as often as not been in denial. But in fact we have made significant progress with acknowledging and addressing limits. With regard to the environment, we increasingly recognize the importance of clean air and water and environmental sustainability more generally, and have made a good start with legislation to protect endangered species. We have become much better at assessing systemic risk than we were a hundred years ago, at least when it comes to systems of an engineering sort. And bit by bit, we are coming to better appreciate basic limits that come with being human—to what we can ultimately know, to what even the best of leadership can often accomplish.

In fact many of the most important advances of the last century have had to do specifically with limits. Of particular pertinence to our inquiry, very often such advances have involved bringing systemic perspective to realms where more machine-like assumptions previously prevailed. Advances that have to do with limits to what we can know, predict, and control have particular significance.

Psychology and psychiatry's new attention to unconscious forces at

the beginning of the last century—most famously with the early contributions of Freud—both anticipated the broader cognition changes that
make culturally mature perspective possible and confronted prevail-
ing realities in particularly consequential ways. Enlightenment thinking promised to bring the whole of understanding and experience into
the sure light of conscious awareness. The idea of an unconscious directly confronted this Modern Age story that made knowing limitless.
Over the last century, psychology has increasingly questioned not just
whether bringing all of understanding into the light of pure reason is
possible, but whether it is anything we would want—a conclusion to
which we will later give more particular attention.[10]

Modern thinking in sociology and anthropology expanded on
psychology's limits-acknowledging picture by emphasizing that what
we understand about others is always as much about ourselves and
how we understand as it is about what we seek to understand. And
while the postmodern argument may stop short of providing detailed
guidance, it has been quite eloquent in describing how old certainties
now fail us.

This new recognition of limits to what we can know and control
went beyond better understanding ourselves as systems. Some of the
most important observations involved how we make sense of our biological and physical worlds. The most advanced thinking in biology
today accepts that living systems can be so complex that outcomes become impossible to predict. It also seriously considers that the question of what makes life alive may be simply unanswerable.[11] In physics, quantum mechanics continually confirms outcomes that defy usual

---

10 In Chapter Four I will describe how intelligence has multiple aspects that
appropriately function at varying levels of awareness. In Chapter Six we
will examine how Cultural Maturity's cognitive changes give awareness an
ultimately more powerful, but also less defining significance.

11 Certainly it remains unanswerable if we limit ourselves to the usual ways
of thinking. Systems theorist Gregory Bateson articulated this conclusion
particularly well (see Bateson, Gregory, *Steps to an Ecology of Mind*, Uni-
versity of Chicago Press, 1972). *Quick and Dirty Answers to the Biggest of
Questions* examines this limitation and proposes that we can get a long way
toward a needed definition if we think of life as a systemically "emergent"
property.

explanation. Werner Heisenberg's Uncertainty Principle (which states that we cannot know a particle's position and momentum simultaneously) gave us one of the earliest[12] and most influential demonstrations of ultimate limits to understanding.

Besides supporting the observation that we have already made real progress with Cultural Maturity's task, each of these limits-related advances also helps confirm the conclusion that maturely engaging real limits makes us more. With none of these advances has the acceptance of real limits diminished our felt sense of potency or our appreciation of the ultimate vitality and order of the world around us.

Limits and Contradiction:
Cultural Maturity's New Common Sense

Easily the most striking thing about these reflections on the ultimate significance of limits is how often they have presented apparent contradiction. The basic idea that acknowledging inviolable limits could be consistent with hope can itself seem contradictory—limits are limitations, after all. And my claim that acknowledging inviolable limits reveals new possibilities could, at first, seem even more contradictory. But both of these outcomes should now make basic sense.

We find a further apparent contradiction in the specific new kind of possibility that comes with a mature systemic engagement of limits. Because it provides important insight into the unique significance of Cultural Maturity's changes, it warrants special attention. That further contradiction: While we appropriately see the new possibilities that come with engaging limits as dramatic—certainly they are essential to going forward in our time, and that is a remarkable outcome—we could also accurately claim that what results from maturely engaging limits is more "ordinary" than what we've known before. In the end, Cultural Maturity's limits-infused picture is about nothing more than better recognizing things for what they are. It is about more accurately seeing what is possible to see—at least with our human eyes.

In fact, with this chapter's reflections, this too makes perfect sense. You've seen how idealized myths of limitlessness protect us with heroic images of specialness and illusionary possibilities. In the end, what

---

12 First articulated in 1927

maturely engaging limits asks is that we surrender our protective illusions and better acknowledge just what is. A successful response to the challenge of limits makes existence newly full and inspiring—but only because existence *is* these things. Goethe wrote that "it is ordained that trees cannot grow to heaven."[13] Culturally mature systemic understanding is about accepting that this is so. It is also about understanding why we would not want it any other way.

A quick summary:

Our times require that we better recognize real limits and respond creatively to them. Cultural Maturity's changes make the needed more mature relationship to limits possible. Culturally mature perspective also reveals how a mature relationship to limits invites options that before we could not have recognized. Ideological beliefs always in some way make claims of limitlessness. Acknowledging real limits helps us step beyond ideology and engage the greater possibility that naturally accompanies mature systemic understanding.

The next two chapters address different kinds of new challenges and capacities, but each also could be summarized in terms of the importance of better acknowledging limits. With Chapter Four, we confront necessary limits to what we can be for others, and also to what other people can be for us. The new picture that results requires that we rethink not just relationship, but human identity. Chapter Five confronts a limit that defines much of what makes Cultural Maturity not just significant in the sense that we see with any new stage in culture's evolution, but of unique consequence. We will examine how fundamental limits exist to continuing on the developmental course that has brought us to this point in human history.

---

13 Goethe, Johann Wolfgang von, *Dichtung and Wahtheit*, 1811-1814

CHAPTER 4

Rethinking Relationship and Identity— Love, Leadership, and the Modern Myth of the Individual

I am large. I contain multitudes.
— WALT WHITMAN

A few questions:

1. What will love look like in the future, with gender roles and relationship expectations today in such flux?
2. How do we best understand the future of leadership?
3. What ultimately does it mean to be an individual, and are there implications in the answer for the future of human identity and the structures of institutions?

Some of Cultural Maturity's most important challenges and needed new capacities have to do with human relationships. When we leave behind culture's parental status, we also necessarily leave behind the familiar relationship rules and assumptions of times past. And Cultural Maturity's deeper changes also affect our experience of relationship. Both of the previous two chapters' main themes—the need to step beyond projection and think more systematically and the importance of leaving behind mythologized images of limitlessness—fundamentally alter the meaning of relationship and what relationships require of us.

These changes in how we engage one another in relationship also help us understand an arguably even more basic concern. Our times require that we rethink human identity. Identity's new meaning similarly follows from where Cultural Maturity's changes take us. Cultural Maturity presents a more multifaceted and complete picture of what it means to be a human being. This chapter addresses both kinds of challenges.

Beyond Romeo and Juliet—The Changing Face of Love

The topic of love might seem out of place in this inquiry. But changes in our experience of love—indeed, in how love works—provide some of the best evidence that today's changing realities represent a new chapter in our human story. The topic of love also presents a particularly personal and graphic illustration of how our times challenge us to rethink not just relationship, but who we are.

As a psychotherapist, I often work with couples. In this work, I find nothing more striking than how deeply love is changing—and few things more gratifying than supporting these changes. We witnessed the beginnings of this evolution with the previous century's unprecedented questioning of traditional gender roles. Today, changes continue. For me, observing how love is changing provides important hope—both for the future of love and for Cultural Maturity's broader realization.

To fully appreciate what is becoming different, we need to start with the whole notion that love is something that in fact does change. People tend to assume that love is an eternal notion—that love is love. And if we do recognize that our ideas about love have evolved, we tend to assume that love as we have known it in our time represents a culminating ideal. In fact, love as we tend to think of it—romantic love—is a relatively recent cultural "invention"—a product of our Modern Age[1]—and, by all evidence, not an end point.

Romantic love is appropriately celebrated. Previously, love's determinations were made by families or by a matchmaker. Romantic love provided an important step forward in love's evolution—toward, among other things, greater authority in our lives. But we should not expect romantic love to be the end of love's story.

We gain perspective by noting that the Modern Age Romeo and Juliet ideal represents something quite different from what we tend to

---

1 We idealized romantic love in the Middle Ages, but that was unrequited love—love held at a safe, abstract distance.

assume it to be about. We tend to think of romantic love as love based on individual choice. But while choice set against the constraints of family expectations is without question much of what makes Romeo and Juliet a compelling tale, romantic love is not yet about individual choice in the sense of loving as separate, whole people.

Previous observations about projection and systemic completeness help clarify why we should expect further chapters in love's story. With romantic love, the bond is created through the projection of parts of ourselves. I ascribe feminine aspects of myself to you; you ascribe masculine aspects of yourself to me. And as always happens with projection, we also mythologize the other, in this case making that person our brave knight or fair lady, our answer and completion (or, at less pleasant moments, the great cause of our suffering). Romantic love is two-halves-make-a-whole love, rather than love between individuals as whole systems.

Up until very recently, these two-halves-make-a-whole mechanisms have served us. Much of the "glue" of relationship—the magnetism of love and the basis of commitment—has come from this giving away of key dimensions of ourselves to the other. These protective mechanisms have not only benefited us, they are what has allowed love to be possible. Making the other our answer has shielded us from uncertainties and complexities that we could not before have tolerated.

But today, love is requiring more of us. Just like we see with the possibility of more Whole-System relationships between nations and social groups, love that works in our time is increasingly of a more Whole-Person (Whole-System at the level of personal choice) sort. Whole-Person love challenges us not just with regard to the stories we tell ourselves about love, but fundamentally—with regard to what love entails, what makes relationship love at all.

In my work as a therapist, I increasingly see people seeking out more Whole-Person bonds—and for good reasons. Whole-Person love offers important rewards. It makes possible a deeper sense of personal identity in relationship. And because it involves bringing more of ourselves to the experience of relationship, it also offers deeper kinds of bonds and more fulfilling ways of being together. I don't see Whole-Person love as some luxury. The future of intimacy depends on our ability to realize this new, fuller kind of connecting.

Whole-Person love doesn't let us off easily. It requires that we know both ourselves and the person we are with more deeply. Also, the new freedoms that come with it mean that we choose between options that are not as clear and obvious as in times past. And of particular significance, love's more Whole-Person picture requires that we accept limits to what we can be for one another. The other person stops being our ultimate answer—and, similarly, we no longer get to be the ultimate answer for them. Love increasingly requires that we recognize how, as Lily Tomlin put it, "we are all in this alone." I've spoken of our Modern Age narrative as heroic. The mythic complement is that it is also romantic. Whole-Person love requires that we leave both halves of this symbolic story in the past.

Successful Whole-Person love hinges both on what we bring to love—the whole of ourselves—and also on the sophistication of thought that comes with culturally mature perspective. Love that surrenders traditional projections requires a more nuanced appreciation of love's workings. We aren't used to thinking this much about love. In fact, thinking and love have often been viewed almost as opposites. But as cultural dictates stop doing much of our thinking for us, we must bring new levels of awareness and discernment to our experience of love. Our times demand—and begin to make possible—a new maturity not just in how we engage love, but also in the subtlety we bring to understanding it.

Here are a few examples of the new kinds of understanding needed for love to work: Whole-Person love require a better appreciation of how love can be different for different people.[2] It also requires a deeper recognition of how love changes and evolves—over the course of a relationship, through our lives, and at least a bit (as here) more culturally. And with gender roles no longer providing the same guidance, we need to be more

---

2 In workshops I've done on personality style differences, one of the most striking observations has to do with the dramatically different cues people of different temperaments use to know if someone loves them. When we are in a relationship with a person of a different personality style from our own, we must be keenly attentive to such differences. (In my work with couples, I find relationships between people who have very different temperaments to be increasingly common. Later, in Chapter Six, I will reflect on why this might be so.)

conscious of the practicalities of how love interplays with other parts of our lives.[3] In the end, success with Whole-Person love requires a deeper and more nuanced appreciation for what makes love love.[4]

We gain added perspective—not just on love, but on Cultural Maturity's broader changes—by noting what culturally mature love is not. Culturally mature love is not some final expression of individualism—or, at least, not this alone. Individualism provides needed separateness, but by itself it teaches us nothing about the needed new depth of connection. Culturally mature love is also fundamentally different from common humanistic ideas about wholeness in relationship. Such notions tend to have less to do with loving as whole people than identification with the emotional side of experience. Nor is Whole-Person love about some postmodern, anything-goes relativism. Culturally mature love requires greater critical discernment, not less.

One of the best indicators of Whole-Person love is what happens if a love relationship ends. Love relationships based on romantic projection don't tend to end pleasantly. The reason is simple: Separation requires that we extract the projected parts of ourselves. Often we create the needed distance by replacing the idealized projections that drew us together with projection of an "evil other" sort.

Whole-Person love relationships tend to end differently. There can be significant sadness and disappointment that things no longer work as before. But very often people remain friends in some way. At the least, there tends to be gratitude for what was shared even if ultimate dreams could not be fulfilled. Notice that this result is again rather common sense. If we were initially attracted to someone, and we have good judgment, that person was probably basically good. The conclusion that he or she has suddenly become an "evil other," if it has any accuracy at all, can only reflect our own failings (that we could have chosen to be with such an evil person in the first place).

---

3 For example, with traditional gender roles, men worked and women stayed at home with the children. With Whole-Person relationship, each couple finds the work/home balance that best fits the two people's personalities and life circumstances.

4 Chapter Five looks at how culturally mature perspective alters the truths we use to guide us, including those we use to guide us in love.

With Whole-Person love, we again encounter what can seem to be contradictions. One is familiar from our look at systemic limits. While Whole-Person love is potentially more powerful than what we have known, it is also in important ways more humble—again more "ordinary." To get there we must give up what often most defined love's excitement in the past—finding someone who could be our answer and completion. With Whole-Person relationship, love becomes more about loving another person for just who they are.

There is also a related seeming contradiction that can seem even more of a surprise, one that is particularly important to Whole-Person love being realizable. While Whole-Person love is decidedly more complex in its demands, there are ways, too, in which Cultural Maturity's changes make love simpler. The soap-opera–like tensions that too often come with romantic love, rather than being intrinsic to the fact of love, reflect interactions between mutually projected parts of ourselves. When love is no longer based on projection, we are able to leave much of love's drama behind us. Whole-Person love can be more dramatic in the sense of being more meaning-filled. But, in the end, Whole-Person love is simply about figuring out how two whole people can best add to each other's lives.[5]

As yet, examples of culturally mature love in the media are rare—romantic titillation and the soap opera melodrama of "reality" television more often prevail. But this should not surprise us given the general cultural immaturity of commercial media. Culturally mature changes in love *are* very much happening. Twenty years ago in my work with couples, it was unusual for the changes of culturally mature love to play a major role. Today, it is unusual if they do not. This makes working with couples today particularly rewarding. It also supports hope that Cultural Maturity's changes more generally are further along than we might think.

Culturally Mature Leadership

While love and leadership might seem to represent very different sorts of concerns, the changes reordering love and leadership have much

---

5 With the next chapter's examination of how Cultural Maturity alters the truths we use to make choices, we will look at how the truths we draw on in all parts of our lives, while more sophisticated, are also ultimately simpler.

in common. We could think of love's changes as having ultimately to do with leadership—with how we make mature choices in our intimate lives. The concept of Cultural Maturity describes how our times require an essential "growing up" in how we understand, relate to, and embody authority. This includes authority of every sort, from that exercised in leading nations; to the expertise of teachers, doctors, or ministers; to the authority we apply in making the most intimate of personal life choices. Here I will focus on leadership of the formal sort.

As with other culturally shared dynamics, formal leadership has evolved over time. Formal leadership's evolution has involved not just what leadership looks like, but what makes it leadership at all. Leadership, as we generally think of it, arrived with our Modern Age— with the emergence of individual determination as a rallying cry and with the rise of democratic principles. New leadership assumptions and approaches then directly challenged the more heredity-based and dictatorial/authoritarian leadership practices of earlier times. But while these changes represented important steps forward, a further chapter in how we conceive of and engage leadership will be essential for times ahead. The reasons are similar to those we saw with love's new realities: We need more Whole-Person/Whole-System kinds of leadership.

Projection's role again helps make sense of both what we have known before and what is changing. Mythologized projection has always before been central to the workings of leadership. We've projected our power onto leaders. This is most obvious with leaders of times well past such as pharaohs and kings, who were seen, if not as gods, then certainly as god-like. But in a similar if not quite so absolutist way, we have continued to make leaders heroic symbols in modern times. We described John Kennedy using the imagery of Camelot. We depicted Ronald Reagan as a mythic father figure. In a related way, we've symbolically elevated not just political leaders, but authorities of all sorts—religious leaders, professors, doctors, and leaders in business. The relationship of leaders and followers has been based on two-halves-make-a-whole systemic dynamics.

Projecting our power onto leaders has served us. As with "chosen people/evil other" projections in relations between social groups, and the romanticized projections of two-halves-make-a-whole intimacy, idealizing authority has protected us from life's easily overwhelming bigness. It has provided a sense of order in a world that would otherwise be too complex and deeply uncertain to tolerate. But as we have seen with other systemic dynamics, going forward will require more than leadership as we have known it. Leadership as traditionally conceived stops short of a full realization of what it means either to be an individual or to exercise authority. If the concept of Cultural Maturity holds, the future depends on the possibility of leadership that more effectively reflects the whole of who we are.

Do we currently see such Whole-Person/Whole-System changes in how we think about and embody leadership? Often the evidence mostly seems to suggest otherwise. Trust in leadership of all sorts today is less than it was at the height of anti-authoritarian rhetoric in the 1960s.

But the implications of this lack of trust may be different than we imagine. We could easily assume—and people have argued—that this modern lack of confidence in leadership reflects something gone terribly wrong—broad failure on the part of leaders, a loss of moral integrity on the part of those being led, or even an impending collapse of society. But this diminishing confidence is also consistent with what we would predict as old forms of leadership give way to more culturally mature possibilities. I think it is not so much that leaders themselves are failing today, than that old forms of leadership are failing. In fact we see changes consistent with the needed, more mature kind of leadership with authority relationships of many sorts. Some of the most important "bridgings" beginning to manifest in our time link the opposite halves of authority-related polarities—teacher and student, doctor and patient, minister and churchgoer, president and populace. They reflect a more mature and systemic leadership picture. Authority relationships of all sorts are becoming more two-way, with more listening and flexibility on the part of leaders and more engaged and empowered roles for those who draw on a leader's expertise and guidance.

Each of the previous chapters' themes offers insight into what becomes different with Cultural Maturity's needed more "grown-up" kind of leadership relationship. As far as projection, culturally mature leadership reincorporates it, or shuns it to begin with. The leader/follower relationship becomes a more expressly human relationship. As far as limits, such leadership confronts an essential further limit I noted earlier with love. It requires that we recognize limits to what one person can be for another—in this case, both what leaders can be for followers and what followers can be for those who lead. Culturally mature leadership is the leadership of good and smart people—leaders and followers—each doing difficult jobs.

Besides altering the leader/follower relationship, culturally mature leadership also requires specific new leadership abilities that follow from the more systemic ways of thinking that inherently accompany it. Such new abilities vary depending on the realm in which leadership is exercised, but some characteristics from the best of current nation-state leadership provide illustration. Such leadership seeks to avoid the kind of polarizing that makes enemies, at home and abroad. It appreciates that questions frequently have multiple, often conflicting aspects and that decision-making is commonly more complex than we might prefer (it does not oversimplify for political gain). It inspires when possible while also acknowledging real uncertainties and limits to what we can sometimes achieve. It does not shy away from hard choices. And it is as concerned with the long term—sometimes the very long term—as it is with the immediate. We see related greater nuance and sophistication in the best of contemporary leadership of all sorts.

Some of the implications of Whole-Person/Whole-System leadership can again seem contradictory. As with mature love, such leadership, while more powerful, is also more "ordinary." Stripped of the idealized parental projections of times past, leadership has become a more humble enterprise. The apparent contradiction that I just described that makes culturally mature love more realizable than we might think also comes into play. While culturally mature leadership is more complicated than past leadership in all that we must take into account, it is also in important ways simpler. When we step beyond heroic/romantic mechanisms, we necessarily bring much more to the leadership task. But at the same time, our actions become more straightforward.

Leadership provides a good illustration of the awkward, in-between place that we so often find ourselves in today when it comes to Cultural Maturity's changes. We tend to be much better at demanding the gift of culturally mature leadership than at knowing what to do with it. We may want leaders to get off their pedestals, but frequently when they attempt to do so, we respect them less, not more. We want leaders to be more transparent, to reveal more of themselves and to make fewer decisions behind closed doors; however, when they do, our first response is often to attack them for their human frailties. But even this awkward, in-between place is a start. And it is a start toward a kind of change that should more and more define human possibility.

Relationship, Culturally Mature Identity, and the Modern Myth of the Individual

The changes that I've described in this chapter have implications not just for love and leadership, but also for relationships of all sorts—such as friendships, relationships between parents and children, and the bonds that give us the experience of community or that link people together in organizations. Relationships of all types, whether between individuals or social systems, today are making a parallel set of demands that can be understood to follow directly from Cultural Maturity's new realties. Increasingly, relationships work when we engage them in Whole-Person/Whole-System ways.

Equally important are the implications that these changes have for how we think about who we are as individuals. Because Whole-Person/Whole-System relationship requires that we reincorporate projections, it also requires us to revisit how we think about human identity. Being an individual must now involve more fully recognizing and holding the whole of our complexity. This means bringing greater systemic coherence to the experience of being an individual. It also means better appreciating how multifaceted the experience of being an individual ultimately is.

This more complex and systemic picture of identity is a central attribute of Cultural Maturity. Walt Whitman's words at the beginning of this chapter capture it poetically, at least as it pertains to personal maturity. The full quote: "I contradict myself. Very well, I contradict myself. I am large. I contain multitudes."[6] The whole-box-of-crayons image captures Cultural Maturity's more complete picture of identity conceptually. With Cultural Maturity, identity involves better holding and making use of the whole box. It is about more fully recognizing and more consciously applying our dynamically multihued human natures.

---

6 Whitman, Walt, *Leaves of Grass* (from "Song of Myself"), David Mackay, Philadelphia, 1900

In Chapter Six we will look at how this new picture of identity follows directly from Cultural Maturity's cognitive changes.

This more multifaceted understanding of identity confronts us with a realization that has striking implications not just for how we think of ourselves, but also for how we think about our human future: The Modern Age picture of individuality—in which we have taken appropriate pride—reflects an ultimately incomplete picture. Creative Systems Theory calls this misconception the modern *Myth of the Individual*. The changing face of relationship that we see with love and with leadership helps us appreciate what has been missing in the old picture and the implications of its absence.

The Myth of the Individual has three parts. First is the Modern Age assumption that we have, in fact, been individuals. I've described how we have thought of both romantic love and modern leadership as expressions of individual choice—indeed, how we have thought of a new freedom for the individual as what, in each instance, made them new and different. A world in which love's determinations were made by family or a matchmaker, along with more authoritarian forms of leadership, gave way to experiencing—indeed, celebrating—choice as being increasingly ours to make. But as we've seen with both love and leadership, this apparent realization of the individual was illusionary, or at least partial and preliminary. In each case, what we saw was two-halves-make-a-whole relationship. Being half of a systemic whole is not yet about being an individual, certainly not in any complete sense.

The second part of the modern Myth of the Individual is the assumption that individuality as we have thought of it represents—again—an end point and ideal. Because such "individuality"—the kind we saw with romantic love and heroic leadership—leaves us short of the kind of relating we need for the future, it can't be either an end point or an ideal. Being an individual takes on a fundamentally different meaning with Cultural Maturity's changes. Individual identity becomes about more consciously holding the whole of our human complexity.

The third part of the modern Myth of the Individual concerns an additional apparent contradiction that brings particular emphasis to the fundamental newness of what we see with relationship's changes. It would be reasonable to assume that individuality, when fully achieved, would finally make us wholly distinct from one another. But while culturally mature love and leadership each involve the ability to stand more fully separate, more consciously engaging the whole of our multifaceted complexity also alters identity by deepening our capacity for connectedness.

I've described how Whole-Person love offers the possibility of more complete and enduring love. Whole-Person/Whole-System leadership in a similar way offers deeper and more authentic engagement between leaders and those the leader represents. This deeper connectedness is in part a product of the simple fact that we now bring the whole of ourselves to the task of relating—and are thus capable of engaging in fuller ways. But there is also a related further factor that follows from just what the whole of ourselves includes that we will examine more closely with later more theoretical reflections. Cultural Maturity makes it possible for us to draw more consciously on parts of ourselves that appreciate that to live is to be connected—and not just to particular individuals, but also in community, with nature, and with existence more generally.

To fully understand this third step, we need to recognize how, along with this deepened capacity for connectedness, it also increases our experience of difference—but now authentic difference, not just separateness. When we engage ourselves in more complete ways, we more deeply engage all that makes us uniquely who we are. We encountered a good example of this dual result with previous reflections on bigotry and what getting beyond bigotry asks of us. I proposed that a culturally mature transcendence of bigotry involves not just better recognizing our commonality, but also becoming more cognizant of ways we may authentically differ. This result pertains to relationships between systems of all sorts—between individuals as systems, certainly, but also between social systems large and small. In Chapter Six, we will examine how the new reality that this third part of the Myth of the Individual reveals—both its greater connectedness and greater authentic difference aspects—follows naturally from Cultural Maturity's cognitive reordering.

Since the Myth of the Individual can seem startling on first encounter, I will quickly summarize it and its implications: In times past, we've imagined ourselves to be distinct while more accurately we were identifying with one half of a larger systemic whole. In this sense, we were in fact not really separate. Whole-Person identity allows us to stand truly separate—for the first time. At once, Whole-Person identity helps us more fully appreciate the whole of who we are. One result is a potential depth of relationship that we have not before known. Another is a new depth of connectedness to ourselves and a fuller appreciation for what makes who we are particular.

The Myth of the Individual has pertinence not just to how we think about relationships and individual identity, but also to how we conceive of human institutions—of all sorts. Common assumptions about government as we know it make a good point of reference. I've described how we tend to think of modern representative government as a culminating ideal. Part of the argument for this conclusion is that modern institutional democracy is "government by the people." By this we mean government as an expression of individual choice. But while Modern Age democracy does involve greater choice than the governmental forms of any earlier cultural stage, if what I've described is accurate, democracy in the sense of whole people taking full responsibility for their choices is something we have not yet witnessed. This would require a further step in our evolution as choice-making beings. We have not yet seen "government by the people" in the mature systemic sense that the concept of Cultural Maturity proposes is now becoming necessary. But if what I have described is accurate, such a next step is fully possible—and is beginning to happen.

Previously I've observed several different Cultural Maturity–related changes that could contribute to a next chapter in government. I think specifically of stepping beyond viewing nation-states (and their institutions) as mythic parents, beginning to set aside ideological polarization and partisan pettiness, and leaving behind mythologized concepts of leadership. We can now add one more that in an important way brings all the others together: Culturally mature governance becomes more authentically government by the people, government as an expression of human identity in its fully mature manifestation.

Multiple Intelligences

I've proposed that a more conscious relationship to our "I contain multitudes" inner natures is key to Cultural Maturity's changes. Certainly it is key to the more complete kinds of relationships and fuller sense of identity possible when we step beyond the Myth of the Individual. Later we will look at how this more conscious relationship to human complexity follows directly from Cultural Maturity's cognitive changes. We will also look at how it is key to culturally mature systemic understanding whatever our topic of interest, and how it is central to what makes Cultural Maturity's changes fundamentally different from those of previous major change points.

But, for now, a general introduction will suffice. In Chapter Three I noted how twentieth century thought in psychology and sociology required us to accept limits to knowing. Over the last century, the initial insight—radical for its time—that much in experience is unconscious, has evolved and filled out in essential ways. The specific ways this insight has changed with time help point toward the emerging, more multifaceted picture.

Initially, people interpreted the observation that much in experience is unconscious in a way that did not fundamentally challenge Modern Age assumptions. They concluded that the task was to use awareness to make the unconscious conscious. Today we recognize increasingly that aspects of ourselves that are variously more and less amenable to conscious scrutiny each have importance. With this further recognition, the task becomes not to be conscious of everything, but to be conscious in such a way that our thoughts and actions are allied in the most purposeful and powerful ways. Many of the polarities I've noted—mind and body, objective and subjective, thoughts and feelings—reflect such contrasting aspects of who we are. The box-of-crayons image highlights the new relationship to this multifaceted picture of understanding and identity that comes with culturally mature perspective.

One of the best ways to think about our whole-box-of-crayons internal complexity is to frame it in terms of intelligence's multiplicity. Today the idea that intelligence is multiple—that it has different aspects that work in very different ways—is basic to psychology, education, and cognitive science. The observation that intelligence has multiple parts that interplay to create our particularly human kind of understanding is most obviously important to better understanding who we are and how cognition works. But as you will see, it is specifically important to making sense of Cultural Maturity's changes, both the cognitive reorganization that produces those changes and how Cultural Maturity's changes make new ways of thinking, relating, and acting possible.

It helps to appreciate how fundamentally the idea that intelligence has multiple aspects has challenged Modern Age belief. The Modern Age task was not just to bring understanding wholly into the light, but specifically into the light of reason. Enlightenment belief made intelligence and rationality one and the same—a conceptual shift that was key to getting beyond the superstitions of medieval thought. But Cultural Maturity and the new demands of our time make clear that we can't stop there. It turns out that no culturally mature concept or capacity is fully understandable with our rationality alone.

The fact that our rationality, even at its most astute, is limited can initially be disorienting. We like to believe that being smart and thinking hard enough will get us to the truth. And we tend to believe that when we are not wholly rational, we are less exact. But success is a great motivator. We find that when we apply the whole of our cognitive complexity in the needed more conscious and integrative fashion, new and even more precise ways of thinking and acting become available to us.

Note one immediate connection between intelligence's more consciously multifaceted picture and how I've spoken of Cultural Maturity. I've described how culturally mature understanding is not just about knowledge, but also about wisdom. Wise decision-making requires that we draw on all parts of our cognitive complexity—our rational minds, certainly, but that can only be a start. Knowledge is quite well captured by rationality alone. Wisdom, however, requires a more multifaceted kind of engagement. It requires that we apply the whole of ourselves as cognitive systems. In the end, it requires, too, that we be sensitive to how we need to draw in different ways on our complex cognitive natures at different times and places.

Formulations that look at intelligence more complexly divide the pie of cognition in a variety of ways. For example, the neurosciences have replaced old images of a single managerial rational brain with a view that recognizes multiple quasi-independent "brains"—in one familiar interpretation, a reptilian brain and a mammalian brain, capped with that thin outer cerebral layer in which we humans take special and appropriate pride. Educational theorists offer an array of interpretations, the most well-known being Howard Gardner's eight-part smorgasbord of intelligences—linguistic, musical, mathematical, spatial, kinesthetic, interpersonal, intrapersonal, and rational.[7] The popular idea that we need to think with "both sides of the brain," while neurologically simplistic, draws our attention to how the task is not just to have lots of intelligences at our disposal, but to find ways in which various aspects of how we make sense of things might more consciously work together.

Creative Systems Theory provides a particularly sophisticated frame for thinking about our diverse ways of knowing that plays a central role in this book's perspective on cultural change. Given this particular pertinence for our inquiry, Creative Systems Theory's approach to dividing up intelligence's complexity is worth an introductory look. Creative Systems Theory proposes that what makes us particular, if not unique, as creatures is our remarkable toolmaking, meaning-making—we could say simply "creative"—capacities. It goes on to describe how our multiple intelligences and the particular ways in which they relate to one another are key to our unique creative capacities being possible.

In Chapter Six we will examine just how this works and also look at how a creative framing of intelligence helps clarify why Cultural Maturity's cognitive reordering produces the changes that it does. For now, a basic introduction to how Creative Systems Theory divides up intelligence will suffice. The theory identifies four basic types of intelligence.[8] For ease of conversation, I will refer to them here as body intelligence, imagination, the emotions, and the rational.

Body intelligence[9] is the language of movement, sensation, and sensuality, as well as other aspects of ourselves that we are only beginning to discover. For example, it is increasingly accepted that the immune system is in the broadest sense "intelligent"; it makes subtle discriminations and learns every day to make new ones.

---

7 Gardner, Howard, *Frames of Mind*, Bantam Books, New York, 1983

8 We could break intelligence's picture down further (and CST does), but four types makes a good compromise between oversimplification and unnecessary complexity.

9 What CST calls *Somatic/Kinesthetic Intelligence*

The intelligence of the imagination[10] gives us the language of poetry, metaphor, dream, and artistic inspiration. In *A Midsummer Night's Dream*, Shakespeare was referring to imaginal intelligence when he wrote, "the lover, the lunatic, and the poet/are of imagination all compact."

The intelligence of our emotions[11] provides the language of mood, affect, and the more interpersonal aspects of discourse. It also relates closely with how impulse translates into action.

Rational intelligence[12] provides the language of "if A then B" syllogistic logic, the more explicit aspects of verbal exchange, and "objective" observation. (I put the word "objective" in quotes because of how, in modern times, we've tended to equate "objective" with "complete." The fact that such observation tends to draw on only part of cognition suggests otherwise and invites a more nuanced interpretation.[13])

Creative Systems Theory proposes that these different ways of knowing represent more than just diverse approaches to processing information. They are the windows through which we make sense of our worlds. Creative Systems Theory also describes how they represent the formative tendencies that lead us to shape our worlds in the ways that we do. Later we will look at how our multiple intelligences function to support and drive our audaciously creative human natures.

A quick summary:

Cultural Maturity's changes alter human relationships of all kinds—both relationships between individuals and the relationships that define larger social groupings. Relationships become of a more Whole-Person/Whole-System sort. Cultural Maturity's changes similarly alter how we think about identity.

---

10 What CST calls *Mythic/Imaginal Intelligence*

11 What CST calls *Emotional/Moral Intelligence*

12 What CST calls *Rational/Material Intelligence*

13 See "Cultural Maturity's Cognitive Changes" in Chapter Six.

Identity takes on a more whole-box-of crayons definition. It both derives a new systemic coherence and comes to better reflect our multifaceted inner makeup. The recognition that intelligence has multiple aspects provides one of the best ways to appreciate this more multifaceted picture and its implications. When we more consciously hold and apply our multiple intelligences, both how we relate and who we think we are change fundamentally.

In the chapter to come, we examine how Cultural Maturity's changes alter not just how we think about and use intelligence, but the truths that we necessarily draw on in making decisions. Beyond Cultural Maturity's threshold, we come to think about truth in fundamentally new ways.

CHAPTER 5

Understanding What Matters and Why— Truth, Responsibility, and the Future of Human Advancement

> *Postmodern man has stopped waiting for Godot.*
> — STEINAR KVALE

A few questions:

1. How do we make good moral decisions without the clear cultural guideposts of times past?
2. Does the information revolution support culturally mature change?
3. How do we best define progress if our actions are to result in real human advancement?

Our final needed new capacity is arguably the most pivotal, but also easily the most difficult to fully grasp. Cultural Maturity requires that we revisit what matters—or we could say, more simply, what makes something true. It does so in two ways: First, as culture's past parental role diminishes in influence, the truths we draw on become more explicitly ours to choose. Second, the more systemic understandings that become available to us allow us to get more directly at what creates significance, and in the process, to think about what matters in more nuanced and sophisticated ways.

In the end, Cultural Maturity challenges us to rethink the truths we use not just in the sense that our conclusions become different, but fundamentally, in the sense of what makes them true at all. It is an outcome suggested by the previous chapter's introduction to multiple intelligences. When we draw more consciously on the whole of our cognitive complexity, our thinking produces not just different answers, but whole new ways of understanding. In the next chapter we will examine this result more closely, along with the cognitive reordering that produces it.

Our interest with this chapter is more basic. With Cultural Maturity, the truths we draw on become fundamentally different in what they ask of us and where they take us. I will describe how stepping over Cultural Maturity's threshold alters the truths we use to guide us in every part of our lives—those that we use in making personal life choices and also those required when making shared human decisions and creating our social institutions.

Of particular importance for this inquiry, I will also address ways in which Cultural Maturity's changing picture of what matters relates to our ideas about what advancing as a species entails. A critical recognition ties directly to my claim that Cultural Maturity involves changes of a kind we have not seen before. There is an important sense in which Cultural Maturity's cognitive changes alter advancement's historical trajectory. This result is essential not just to the possibility of more mature ways of thinking and acting, but also to the option of going forward at all.

Personal Truth

Let's start with the truths we necessarily draw on in making personal life decisions. At the least, such truths require that we assume greater responsibility. Ultimately, this is a double kind of responsibility, not just for the choices we make, but also for more deeply addressing what makes a choice good.

The first aspect of this needed new responsibility is easiest to see: Our choices become more specifically our own. With the diminishing influence of cultural guideposts, personal truths of all sorts—what we personally choose to believe, our personal values, the directions in which we decide to take our lives—become more expressly personal. Moral decision-making in today's world provides an example I will come back to throughout these truth-related reflections. Without the secure cultural guidance of times past, we become newly responsible in the sense that moral determinations are more directly ours to make.

In a way, this first aspect of the needed new responsibility continues a familiar progression. Antoine de Saint-Exupery proposed that "To be a man (person) is precisely to be responsible."[1] Each stage in culture's evolution has conferred greater personal authority—the age of kings more so than that of god-kings, our modern age of the individual more so than that of royal decree.

But while in a sense familiar, this first aspect of the needed new responsibility is also wholly new. While we've witnessed greater personal authority, and thus increasing freedom of choice, with each new chapter in culture's story, culture's major truths have always before remained assumed—and assumed to be unchanging. Our religious, political, and scientific certainties have continued to shield us from magnitudes of responsibility that would have been impossible to endure. With the diminishing influence of traditional guideposts, in a new and increasingly explicit sense, choice comes to lie in our individual human hands.

The second aspect of the new responsibility is not so immediately obvious, but it is just as critical if our choices are to have real substance—if they are to reflect anything more than postmodern arbitrariness. In a whole new sense, we become responsible for reaching deeply into ourselves to determine on just what we should base our decisions. We can't stop with a loss of traditional guideposts. If we are to make useful choices going forward, we must more explicitly engage what, uniquely for us, makes a thought or act significant. Turning again to moral decision-making for illustration, if today's greater freedom to choose is to have any real meaning—to be anything more than an empty moral relativism—we must plumb our experience and engage basic questions of what for us makes a choice moral.

This second aspect of the needed new responsibility is fundamentally new—new in the sense that we've not witnessed anything like it before. But it is increasingly becoming not just necessary, but also something we are capable of. In Chapter Six, we will examine how the

---

1 Saint-Exupéry, Antoine de, *Terres des Hommes*, Reynal and Hitchcock, 1939

cognitive changes that give us Cultural Maturity's new kind of systemic perspective make this new and greater depth of engagement possible.

Personal choice–related examples from previous chapters highlight this second kind of new responsibility—at the least its necessity. A rewarding life as a man or a woman today requires more than just a willingness to question past gender dictates. Along with this, it demands a new and deeper relationship to ourselves as gendered beings. Similarly, success in love has come to require more than just confronting past assumptions and allowing the possibility of new options. It has also come to demand a deeper and more direct appreciation for the needs that love fulfills (companionship, intimate bonds, parental cooperation, and so on). In a related way, a fulfilling sense of identity requires not just that we challenge past cultural expectations but, in addition, that we draw on a more personal and complete relationship to the question of what for us creates worth.

The developmental analogy again provides helpful associations. Decision-making with second-half-of-life maturity in personal development in a more limited way also involves both parts of this double kind of responsibility. It requires that we stand back from our choices and question earlier personal assumptions—of particular pertinence for the analogy, that we step back from assumptions we might have acquired from our parents. And personal maturity also similarly requires that we plumb more deeply into ourselves and examine afresh just what we wish to base our decisions on. The potential for greater wisdom that comes with second-half-of-life maturity has its roots in this second kind of process.

With cultural as opposed to personal maturity, this double kind of responsibility applies to every choice we make. It also involves a more fully penetrating kind of engagement with the whole of ourselves as systems than has before been needed—or been an option. We've seen the consequences of this two-part process with previous reflections. In the end, it is this combination of stepping back and deeper engagement that allows us to leave behind "chosen people/evil other" projections; effectively address limits; and engage relationships, identity, and intelligence in more complete ways.

In the end, the new kind of truth that Cultural Maturity's double responsibility produces is more fully systemic not just in the sense of being more encompassing; it is also more reflective of the particular kind of systemic vitality that makes us human. The box-of-crayons metaphor points toward this result. I've described how culturally mature understanding requires that we better take the whole box of crayons into account. This involves both stepping back so we can better appreciate the whole box—including its "creative" implications. It also involves more deeply engaging all that we see so that we are able to draw more directly on our uniquely multifaceted—dynamically "multihued"—systemic natures.

The box-of-crayons image also highlights something else of major importance for our inquiry that we will later examine more closely. It brings attention to how successfully taking on this double responsibility makes multiple new kinds of discernment—really, whole new kinds of truth—both possible and necessary. We can draw again on moral decision-making in today's world for examples.

First come necessary "whole-box" discernments. I've described how today's weakening of moral guideposts means that along with taking new responsibility for our choices, we also need to think more directly in terms of what makes an act moral. We can summarize what addressing moral truth more directly asks of us with a simple whole-box observation. We need to more directly determine the degree to which an act is life-affirming (or more specifically, human life-affirming).[2] This kind of determination requires that we consciously draw on the whole of who we are as living human beings—all the crayons in the box. My previous reflections on the role of multiple intelligences provide a ready reference. We can't make this kind of discernment with our rationality alone. The only tool that can get at moral truth at its most basic is the whole of our own living, human cognitive complexity. Chapter Six looks at several examples of this "whole-box" kind of systemic determination.[3]

---

2 In an important sense, the degree to which an act is life-affirming is what moral truth has always been about. The difference between now and times past is that prior to now, culturally specific moral dictates have provided shared, once-size-fits-all shorthands for this kind of determination.

3 Creative Systems Theory calls such "whole-box" distinctions *Whole-System Patterning Concepts*.

But making such "whole-box" discernments—getting at truth at its most basic—can only be a start. We must also learn to more consciously apply the various crayons and recognize their particular contributions. We need to bring new detail to the truths we use. In particular, we need more detailed truths that help us address systemic context and contingency.

We can turn once more to the moral decision-making example for illustration. If any single assertion captures the heart of moral truth, it is the Golden Rule: "Do unto others as you would have them do unto you" (a whole-box measure). But when we step over Cultural Maturity's threshold, we quickly begin to see how profoundly the Golden Rule depends on context. Different people will want different things "done unto" them—as a function of cultural stage, upbringing, personal style, and more. Culturally mature moral decision-making requires not just that we address morality at its most basic, but also that we always be sensitive to the multiple-crayons-in-the-box nature of what ultimately makes an act life-affirming.

In Chapter Six, we will look more closely at this more detailed and specific kind of systemic distinction. But observations in previous chapters have at least suggested the importance of such greater attention to context. I have described how addressing love more directly than was necessary with the more role-defined love relationships of times past is just a first step, how culturally mature love also requires that we learn to make more detailed discernments. At the least, culturally mature love requires greater self-knowledge and a greater sensitivity to our potential partner's uniqueness. But, in the end, it also requires more particular contextual sensitivities; for example, to how love can be different for people of different personality styles and at different times in any one person's life. In a similar way, culturally mature leadership requires not just that we engage leadership's tasks in a way that is more straightforward. It also requires new, more context-specific recognitions—for example, about how what effective leadership requires of us can be very different with different kinds of leadership tasks, how leadership demands can change over time, and how human differences—differences in background, skills, temperament, or overall capacity—can dramatically alter the demands of good leadership.

The importance of recognizing context-specific truths applies not just to particular concerns such as love and leadership, but also to crafting overarching approaches to understanding that can help us make this kind of observation. The developmental framework that gives us the concept of Cultural Maturity represents one such overarching approach. We see another reflected in my earlier assertion that ideological beliefs involve taking one crayon in the systemic box and making it the whole truth. Any approach to systemic understanding that can help us going forward must be able to address both temporal (time-specific) and more here-and-now contextual variables.[4]

It is important to clearly distinguish the new relationship with truth that comes with Cultural Maturity's changes from outcomes that might seem similar. Certainly, the result is very different from some final expression of Modern Age Enlightenment objectivity. The kind of systemic understanding we are interested in is more complete, but it is not about some final clarity. Many of the parts of ourselves that culturally mature perspective draws on defy ready depiction, and uncertainty—limits to what we can know—necessarily comes with the territory. What we encounter is also wholly different from some simplistic, different-strokes-for-different-folks moral relativism. It is about bringing greater ultimate precision to human decision-making, not less. Culturally mature truth in our individual lives is about choosing in ways that better honor our own multifaceted complexities. It is also about better appreciating the deep complexities that order the world in which we must make our personal choices.

Shared Truths

Cultural Maturity's changes alter the choices we make together—in our professions, our communities, and in culture as a whole—in similar ways. Cultural Maturity again requires that we take new responsibility, in this case for the truths we draw on as social beings. And once again this is necessarily a double responsibility, one that requires not just that we more consciously choose, but also that we engage our human complexity with a directness and depth that has not before been an option.

---

4 Creative Systems Theory calls "crayon-particular" discernments of the temporal sort *Patterning in Time* concepts, and more here-and-now contextual discernment concepts *Patterning in Space*. (See "'Creative Systems' Understanding" in Chapter Six.)

Cultural Maturity makes us more deeply responsible for crafting good laws—and it also requires us to bring a fuller kind of perspective to our understanding of what makes a good law good. It makes us more deeply responsible for making profitable economic decisions—and at once, it requires that we ask in more encompassing ways what it means to profit. It makes us more immediately responsible for establishing sound international policy—and, at the same time, it makes us responsible for more consciously determining what kind of world we want our policies to produce.

And on all of these fronts, we again need new truths of both of the new systemic sorts that our box-of-crayons image suggests. We need "whole-box" systemic truths, truths that better get at all that goes into making something true. And we also need more crayon-particular truths that help us engage detail and context. If we are to make effective collective decisions in times to come, we need ways of thinking about what matters that are more encompassing than we have known before, and we also need approaches to understanding that help us be more sensitive to how multifaceted what matters can be.

Along with bringing specific shared truths into question, culturally mature perspective also challenges us to rethink the assumptions on which we base the structures of our institutions. Cultural Maturity requires us to think in more systemic ways about how institutions work and to re-imagine institutions in more dynamic and complete ways. We've touched previously on a couple of examples: the importance of revisiting the assumptions of modern health care and of democratic government as we have known it.

Rethinking health care and government each necessarily involve both parts of our needed new double responsibility. With each, we need to step back, question old assumptions, and accept a more fundamental kind of responsibility for them as institutions. We also need to engage more deeply with what each kind of institution is ultimately about. And in keeping with culturally mature truth's more whole-box-of-crayons picture, in each case, the new more systemic picture that results is at once more encompassing, and also more particular and multifaceted.

With our look at health care limits, I described how modern medicine's bottom-line measure has been to defeat death and disease—essentially at any cost—and also how, when we step beyond Cultural

Maturity's threshold, this definition stops being sufficient. The new picture is more conscious and also more systemic. It better takes into account all the diverse factors that contribute to human well-being— the whole systemic "box," and also its multiple interrelated "crayons." I've described how health care's new picture, at its best, emphasizes prevention as explicitly as treatment; acknowledges quality of life along with the fact of life; gives attention to psychological, social, and spiritual aspects of health and healing in addition to the purely physical; and recognizes the importance not just of individual health, but also broader societal health. This more systemic picture in the end alters not just health care priorities and how medicine is practiced, but also how health care is understood in relation to culture as a whole.

In a similar way, culturally mature perspective challenges us to reexamine government fundamentally and to entertain the possibility of a new chapter in how we think about it. This requires that we step back and look afresh not just at the structures of government, but also more deeply—at governance and our evolving human relationship to it. The resulting new picture is again more systemic. It involves more encompassing (whole-box) truth discernments—at the most big-picture level, addressing government's purpose, and in particular, its appropriate purpose in our time. It also requires that we bring newly detailed understandings to what good governmental decision-making involves (the pertinent crayons). My previous systemic observations—from the importance of stepping beyond the need for "evil empires" to the necessity of more Whole-Person leadership, to the possibility of governance that more truly reflects "government by the people"—only hint at what a next chapter in governance's story might look like. But again, we see a picture that is both more systemically encompassing, and more dynamically multifaceted than how we have thought about institutions in times past.

Cultural Maturity's changes challenge and stretch the underlying assumptions of every sphere of understanding—education, science, religion, art, and more (as I explore in other writings[5])—and they do so

---

5   See *The Creative Imperative, Cultural Maturity: A Guidebook for the Future, Quick and Dirty Answers to the Biggest of Questions,* or any of the Creative Systems Theory websites (www.CreativeSystems.org).

in related ways. Later in this chapter, I will describe briefly how Cultural Maturity's changes similarly require that we rethink the truths on which we base economic decisions and economic structures.

Rewriting Our Cultural Narrative

Shared truth reflections have one further essential layer, that which this book is most directly about. We need to rethink the truths that ultimately guide us as a species—our big-picture cultural narratives.

Our cultural stories describe what, at particular cultural times and places, matters to us most—in the end, what for us most makes things true. This way of framing belief reflects a more "psychological" way of thinking about culture than we are used to. But ultimately, the concept of Cultural Maturity is about the "psyche of culture," about who we are collectively and how we make sense of our worlds.

Cultural Maturity's new story is different from cultural narratives of times past in the same basic ways we've seen with both more personal new-truth tasks and smaller-scale shared determinations. First, it demands a newly conscious responsibility in its writing. The framers of the U.S. Constitution were certainly conscious of the newness of what they were doing and its importance as a human accomplishment. But it is also true that they were religious men who retained the reassuring belief that their task was divinely ordained. As today we write our new cultural story, in a more fundamental sense, we are on our own.[6] Second, the new story requires a newly possible depth of attention to questions of what creates significance—now, and in an important sense, ultimately. Again, this demands attention both to truth's big picture and to its context-specific particulars.

Truth's new double responsibility at this most encompassing of scales defines today's overarching shared task. I came of age in the 1960s. The analogous shared task then was to question established truths and established authority. Important new freedoms resulted. The generations that will come of age in this century confront an arguably more

---

6 This doesn't mean that such inventing is done wholly from scratch or on a whim. If the developmental picture we have drawn on here is correct, our task reflects a larger order, just order of a more mortal, expressly human sort.

difficult, but also ultimately even more interesting and consequential task. Today's task is to once again find order and meaning, but not in the old sense of external dictates, and also not just in the form of new freedoms—new freedoms, by themselves, offer no escape from a post-modern, anything-goes world. The new task is to find meaning and order through an increasingly possible, more systemic engagement with all that goes into creating human importance. Not just human fulfillment, but very possibly our survival as a species depends on our success at this most encompassing new-truth task.

This last claim might seem extreme, but without an effective guiding narrative, we lack needed measures—yardsticks—on which to base our choices. This includes choices on which our future well-being depends. Without a compelling narrative to guide us, we can also simply lose hope. I've made reference to our modern crisis of purpose. Today's world offers almost unlimited options, but it can also feel arbitrary, almost random. It can be unclear whether choices matter at all.

Let's take a moment with an example that helps put these circumstances and their implications in perspective. It highlights the critical importance of articulating a new cultural narrative. It also points to how fragile our relationship to needed new truths can be in these transitional times.

People often ask me whether I think the information revolution supports Cultural Maturity's changes. My answer is yes and no. Digital technologies have great potential to support needed changes—by linking us together in new ways, by providing access to information and learning, and by helping to stimulate innovative thinking. But Information Age advances equally have the potential to undermine exactly what our human future most depends on. Which result we see will depend directly on how effectively we articulate what matters going forward.

Throughout history, new technologies have presented risks as well as benefits. The invention of the automobile, the first use of electricity, even the initial harnessing of fire required attention to potential dangers as well as new possibilities. The importance of articulating a new cultural narrative comes into high relief with the recognition that new information technologies present a particularly consequential kind of two-edged-sword challenge. While digital technologies can powerfully serve us, at the same time they can readily become little more than sources of artificial stimulation that function as substitutes for real meaning.

This dynamic is easiest to see with the more simplistic of video games where the repeated visceral excitation of things blowing up serves as the game's ultimate purpose and reward. But it can also manifest in less obvious forms: Take, for example, how social media, while capable of being used to great benefit, can also have us confuse the most trivial kind of "connectedness" with real human relationship. All too often with the digital revolution we find the most superficial of experiences—indeed, what is often, in effect, little more than undifferentiated stimulation—masquerading as significance.

Such confusion of pseudo-significance with meaning is most obviously of concern because it can result in impoverished lives. But there is also a deeper, more ultimate kind of concern. Particularly when the reward is little more than empty stimulation, what we see reflects the same mechanisms that underlie the attractiveness of addicting drugs. The information revolution has the potential equally to catalyze needed changes or to exploit today's lack of guideposts and feelings of randomness by providing us with ever more powerful electronic "designer drugs."

This situation ties to the task of determining and articulating a new cultural narrative in a couple of key ways. First, the measures that a new narrative provides serve as the necessary bases for making the decisions that using new information technologies for positive ends depends on. To apply information technologies wisely, we must effectively discern when particular applications add to or subtract from human significance. This requires having ways of thinking about what comprises significance in our time. A new guiding story, in helping to point us forward, also provides needed measuring sticks for what matters and what does not.

The second way in which this situation ties to the task of new cultural narrative involves how fragile our relationship to needed new truths can often be. Success with discerning where digital technologies in fact benefit us has implications not just for how we use invention, but also for our ability to make good decisions, period—in all parts of life. We've seen how making determinations without reliable cultural guideposts requires a more direct kind of engagement with our internal complexities. Every time we accept the substitution of artificial excitation for meaning, we do critical damage to the internal capacities needed to make good choices—as individuals, and as a species.

How effective we are at addressing the digital revolution's fork-in-the-road challenge will, in the end, have less to do with the technologies themselves, than with how successfully we are at articulating a new cultural narrative and taking on the double responsibility that doing so entails. It will also depend on the commitment we bring to making that new narrative manifest in all parts of our lives. This represents a level of collective responsibility not before required of us.

Today we live in a time of overlapping narratives, and are only beginning to recognize how deeply something new is needed. The Modern Age narrative—in which truth takes the form of juxtaposed heroic and romantic answers—is still very much a part of the stories we tell. As often today, a postmodern narrative prevails—with its emphasis on multiple options, irony, and an absence of final answers. But increasingly, people are appreciating that further steps will be essential.

Here we've looked at the concept of Cultural Maturity as a potential candidate for that needed new narrative—and hopefully by this point, a compelling one. The concept of Cultural Maturity directly addresses the needed double responsibility. It describes stepping back and becoming more conscious of both what means to be human and what ultimately matters in the human experience. Big picture, it provides a way to think about significance that effectively replaces notions that today serve us less and less well—such as the American dream, often-conflicting religious teachings, and progress's picture of unending technological achievement.

Culturally mature perspective also supports the development of more specific new-truth concepts. The new kinds of understanding that come with Cultural Maturity's changes help make all the more particular "whole-box" distinctions that I have described in this chapter possible. They also help put "crayon-specific" particulars of all sorts in context—both context in the temporal sense of how realities change over time, and context in the sense of how here-and-now aspects of the human experience fit together. The concept of Cultural Maturity describes the possibility of again having guideposts—though now of a different, more responsibility-demanding, complexity-acknowledging sort than we have known in times past.

If there are better ways to think about what the future asks of us than what the concept of Cultural Maturity provides, they must accomplish related ends. They must similarly reflect deep acceptance of ultimate responsibility for both our actions and the truths we collectively apply. And they must both provide effective general guidance for going forward and support the development of detailed and life-affirming conceptual tools able to help us make our way.

Rethinking Progress and the Dilemma of Trajectory

The temporal, change-related aspect of Cultural Maturity's new narrative includes a critical result that is key to making full sense of the times we live in. This result makes especially clear how the changes described by the concept of Cultural Maturity are not just important, but inescapably necessary. It also helps us make sense of how Cultural Maturity's changes are particular, different fundamentally from what we have seen before. And it sets the stage for a fuller appreciation of the mechanisms that produce Cultural Maturity's deeper and more complete engagement with significance.

We've made a good start with examining how Cultural Maturity's changes are essential. With the themes of Chapter Two and Chapter Three—leaving behind our past need to project negative parts of ourselves onto others and better acknowledging real limits—we saw how Cultural Maturity's more systemic narrative is necessary if we are to avoid calamity. With Chapter Four's look at engaging human relationships and human identity in more Whole-Person/Whole-System ways, we examined significance that had most obviously to do with new possibility. But because such possibility represents an essential aspect of today's "change whose time has come" picture, in the end, it is similarly critical to a future that we experience as purposeful and hopeful. In this chapter, I've emphasized how the concept of Cultural Maturity provides truths that can guide us going forward. This additional piece is certainly important if we are to move forward at all safely and effectively.

But tied to each of these observations is an even more ironclad argument for the conclusion that changes at least similar to those described by the concept of Cultural Maturity are imperative. In an important structural sense, going forward as we have has simply stopped being an option. Creative Systems Theory calls this the *Dilemma of Trajectory*. The Dilemma of Trajectory describes limits to how far culture's story as we have conceived it—not just recently, but at any time in the past—can take us. Even if we accept that a new chapter in culture's story is needed, we also have to recognize that the direction that has gotten us to where we have come cannot, simply in some new form, get us to where we need to go.

To fully understand the Dilemma of Trajectory, it helps to put our human narrative in motion and think of our human story specifically in terms of advancement. The concept of progress does just this. Progress represents an especially pivotal kind of "truth" measure. It asks how, collectively, at a particular time, we most appropriately conceive of "more." When a time's definition of progress ceases to work, it becomes the opposite of progress—it undermines advancement, serves to make us less. Arguably, today this has become the case.

Our familiar definition of progress has brought untold wonders— institutional democracy, modern economic structures, and dramatic technological advances from the printing press, to the steam engine, to today's computer revolution. But projected into the future unaltered, progress as we have thought of it becomes questionable at best. The obvious sorts of risks such as how increased global competition could inflame conflict and how the violation of planetary environmental limits could put us in great peril are clearly important. But the greatest dangers are more basic. They have to do with progress itself, or at least with how we have thought about it.

The need to fundamentally rethink our modern definition of progress is a responsibility we are only now beginning to accept. In the 1950s we might have asked whether we would succeed at progressing ("Can we beat the Russians to the moon?"). But it is extremely unlikely that we would have asked about progress itself. Today, it is becoming increasingly essential that we do just that. Progress itself is not the issue. In the sense of increasing capacity and possibility, progress will only become more important. But the Dilemma of Trajectory makes continuing forward as we have really not an option.

Let's take a closer look. Through history, how we have thought of "more" has followed a generally understandable, if sometimes bumpy, "onward-and-upward" progression. With each past chapter in culture's story we have witnessed increasing individual freedom, human authority, and technological prowess. The advent of agriculture offered the option of new and more diverse kinds of human activity. The Magna Carta affirmed basic human privilege. And our Modern Age has continued such appropriately proud advancement, indeed provided a kind of culminating expression of it. Modern Age belief celebrates a perceived final realization of individual identity and free will, ultimate dominion over the irrational in ourselves and over the natural world, and ever more wondrous invention as the solution to our problems.

But continuing to cling to the past's onward-and-upward narrative presents fundamental problems. We confront contradictions that usual ways of thinking leave us unable to address. While what we have reaped, and will continue to reap, from culture's evolution toward ever-greater individuality is profound, the future clearly as much cries out for a new appreciation of ways in which we are related—for a fresh understanding of caring, community, and the common good. And while our ever-greater human authority—over nature, over our own bodies, over life's deep mysteries—has similarly had immense significance, in a related way today, its opposite is arguably as much part of what is needed—a new humility to what we cannot control, a new sensitivity to when we should be listening as opposed to directing (whether the voice needing attention is the natural world, our tissues, or the unfathomable). And while ever more complex and wondrous inventions and technologies will certainly play a major role in shaping our human future, in parallel with these other observations, just as important for our well-being will be greater appreciation for the limits of technology as a human solution and an ever-deeper commitment to assuring that what we create serves ultimate good.

On confronting such apparent contradiction, a person could equally conclude that culture's job is to go forward and that its job is to go back. Indeed, the ideas of many well-intentioned people can suggest that going back is the answer. We often hear overt claims of that sort with the more radical of religious and spiritual ideologies and at least statements that romanticize the past in some of the more extreme of liberal/humanist, feminist, and environmental positions. Many debates about the future become little more than games of tug-of-war between these two equally insufficient options. Any concept of the future that can provide substantive guidance for the leadership tasks ahead must be able to resolve this apparent contradiction. Without a way to reconcile the Dilemma of Trajectory, we are at a dead end.

A couple of themes I've touched on previously—the role of polarity in how we think and the fact of multiple intelligences—provide a more specific kind of evidence for the Dilemma of Trajectory. They point toward how continuing forward as we have would sever us from much of what most makes us human. They also point directly toward how Cultural Maturity's changes offer an antidote. We will look at how each applies to the Dilemma of Trajectory in greater detail in the next chapter. For now, they help solidify the concept.

History teaches us that polarity has evolved in a consistent and predictable way through each previous chapter in culture's story.[7] One thing we see with this evolutionary progression is ever-increasing distinction between polar opposites—for example, between humankind and nature, between mind and body, and between the individual and the collective. While always before this direction of change has benefited us—indeed it has been key to all of culture's great advances— it really can't continue. A further distancing of ourselves from nature, our bodies, or the collective would have dire consequences.

The recognition that intelligence has multiple aspects further highlights the Dilemma of Trajectory. In Chapter Six we will look at how each stage in culture's evolution has drawn preferentially on specfic kinds of intelligence. I've noted how the Enlightenment's grand goal was to bring the whole of understanding not just into the light, but into the light of pure reason. In the Modern Age, reason—in combination with a lesser, essentially decorative contribution from more subjective aspects of intelligence—came to define not just intelligence, but truth. Going further in this direction can't work. At the least there is how the sophistication of understanding needed for the future must reflect not just knowledge—which rationality does well—but also wisdom. But

---

7 Creative Systems Theory maps this evolution. See *The Creative Imperative* or *Quick and Dirty Answers to the Biggest of Questions*.

there is also a related more dramatically consequential observation that I will address in the chapter to come. Continuing forward as we have would eventually disconnect us from essential aspects of intelligence. We would not do well without the emotional sensitivities essential to relationship, the power of imagination that lies at the heart of art, or the more primitive aspects of human sensibility so central to a pleasurable and healthy existence.

For this inquiry, as important as recognizing the Dilemma of Trajectory is appreciating how Cultural Maturity's changes reconcile it. The observation that Cultural Maturity's changes make more systemic understanding possible—and in particular make possible systemic understanding of the newly sophisticated and complete sort needed to address our living human natures—directly supports this conclusion. And what we see today with polarity and with intelligence's more encompassing new picture each help make this integrative result more explicit. I've proposed that a defining characteristic of culturally mature systemic perspective is that it "bridges" the polar assumptions of times past. "Bridging" in the sense that takes us over Cultural Maturity's threshold offers a way beyond the Dilemma of Trajectory's seemingly inviolable constraints. Cultural Maturity's cognitive changes also give us a new, at once more conscious and complete relationship to our multiple intelligences. Our multihued, whole-box-of-crayons systemic picture is the result. With this new, more embracing relationship to our multiple intelligences, in another way, we see the Dilemma of Trajectory resolved.

In Chapter Six we will return to the analogy between maturity in our personal lives and Cultural Maturity and more closely examine how it supports this explicitly integrative outcome. We will also look more closely at the cognitive reordering that produces culturally mature perspective and the kind of systemic understanding that results. These additional reflections will add further substance to this chapter's quick-sketch description of the Dilemma of Trajectory. They will also provide additional evidence for my claim that culturally mature perspective effectively takes us beyond the Dilemma of Trajectory. If this claim is accurate, not only do the kinds of changes described by the concept of Cultural Maturity provide a way forward, they may provide the only real option for going forward.

Redefining Wealth

Earlier I promised to return for a brief look at how Cultural Maturity's changes challenge us to rethink the economic sphere. The topic of wealth—how we conceive of it and also the place it holds in our personal and collective lives—brings together questions about personal truth and collective-truth concerns like progress. It also further highlights the Dilemma of Trajectory and what will be required to reconcile it.

The concept of Cultural Maturity emphasizes the importance of defining wealth and profit in more systemically complete ways. We often hear critiques of capitalism, at least as currently practiced. But capitalism itself is just a way of keeping track of resources we exchange. Defining wealth and profit in more systemically complete ways alters what we value most in what we exchange. It also encourages us to make the rules of exchange most in keeping with systemic benefit. In the process, capitalism comes to have quite different implications.

Redefining wealth and profit presents a particularly pivotal example of the needed reexamination of truth this chapter has been about. We like to think of the economic sphere as objective and pragmatic, but if there is one realm of shared human activity that in our time we have deified, it is this. We can think of money as our time's defining ideology. We've come to measure both personal and social well-being almost entirely in economic terms—such as individual "net worth," and rising GNP (a strictly monetary measure).

Culturally mature perspective does not condemn the fact that in modern times we've mythologized money, made it our god. The great advances of the Modern Age would not have been possible without modernity's newly individualist and materialist values. But as with our Modern Age definition of progress, we have begun to recognize that we can't stop there. We are seeing how empty materialism is a major contributor to the loss of hope and purpose so common in our time. We are also beginning to appreciate how a solely material yardstick is inadequate for measuring the health of societies—or even the stability of economies.

If we are to successfully re-conceive our relationship to wealth and money, it helps to recognize that we have done so before, though less consciously. Our Modern Age assumptions were preceded by quite different beliefs. Indeed, from the perspective of the Middle Ages or tribal times, we would likely find modern material values both confusing and unacceptable. Material wealth had significant influence in the Middle Ages, but simple greed was considered one of the seven deadly sins. And in tribal societies the difference is even more pronounced—there is no room for individual advantage that threatens the well-being of the group. Recognizing these differences is important not just because it reminds us that our relationship to wealth and money has changed before. Much of the antipathy that non-Western peoples can feel for Western values lies in these differences, which can be perceived as deeply moral distinctions.

The concept of Cultural Maturity directly challenges our Modern Age ideological relationship to money. It does not advocate for some opposite "small is beautiful" conclusion—which in the end is just an alternative form of ideology. But it does call for rethinking collective and personal wealth in ways that more fully take into account all that creates human meaning, and more specifically, all that human meaning asks of us in our particular time.

The concept of Cultural Maturity argues that today's needed reevaluation is essential not just so that our world will be more fair and so that our values will more fully reflect all that matters to us. Such rethinking will be critical if our economic systems are to work at all. In another way, we confront our Dilemma of Trajectory. Continuing on as we have will more and more often create dangerously unstable, house-of-cards economic realities.

The 2008-2009 financial collapse (in the United States, but ultimately around the globe) at least suggests this result. We appropriately ask just what caused it. Was it simple greed and incompetence? Or perhaps its origins lay with the unfortunate "perfect storm" of economic cycles, globalization, and other hard-to-predict contributors? Mulitple factors likely played roles, but something deeper was certainly also at work. I suspect that the more basic contributor was ideological. ("Ideology," as I use the word here, refers not to liberal or conservative economic theories, but rather to commonly held beliefs about money itself.) If ideology in this sense was not a primary driver, it is very difficult to understand how the best economic and political minds—and almost all of us—could have been blind to what was, in hindsight, a reality inevitably headed for calamity. Neither self-interest nor simple ignorance ultimately explains why events unfolded as they did.

It is remarkable how much the experts failed to see. Certainly they missed how deregulation had created perverse incentives that changed how those in the financial sphere behaved. The financial meltdown has commonly been attributed to investment bankers taking unwise risks. But in most cases, loans that went bad really weren't risks—for them. Bankers would profit pretty much whatever happened. And the short-sightedness ultimately reached even further. Economists—and most everyone else—were in denial about the fact that housing prices could go down as well as up. Any look at history demonstrates that this not only happens, it is inevitable given enough time. All that was needed for the cascade of events that transpired was for housing prices to go down 10 percent. Prices eventually went down nationally an average of 30 to 40 percent, and the cascade became an avalanche.

How could people be so blind—and I include very smart people? In 2004, then-chairman of the U.S. Federal Reserve Alan Greenspan proclaimed "Not only have individuals become less vulnerable to shocks from underlying risk factors, but also the financial system as a whole has become more resilient"[8]—this specifically in reference to highly interlinked financial instruments, such as derivatives, that played a central role in the eventual meltdown. (Some people did anticipate the problem. Warren Buffet warned that derivatives were "financial weapons of mass destruction carrying dangers, that while latent, are potentially lethal."[9]) It is forgivable that economic experts did not accurately forecast just when an economic downturn might occur. But that the greater portion of economic minds did not recognize fundamental instabilities—in hindsight, glaring ones—suggests a kind of blindness more deeply rooted than just ignorance or self-interest. That deeper blindness is a product of our time.

I've described how redefining wealth and profit not only alters what we most value in what we exchange, but also encourages us to make

---

8 From a speech given to the American Bankers Association on October 5, 2004

9 From the Annual Letter to Shareholders of Berkshire Hathaway in 2002

the rules of exchange more in keeping with systemic benefit. Culturally mature perspective doesn't view the "masters-of-the universe" belief that unfettered free markets can be self-regulating as inherently crazy, just simplistic and now dangerously outdated. What it does do is make abundantly clear that such systemically partial belief cannot continue to benefit us. At the very least, the claim that such a worldview is sufficient makes us vulnerable to dismissing—or not even seeing—potential risks. In the end, it leaves us short of the maturity of perspective we need for a future that can work at all. I quote Thomas Friedman from a New York Times article written in the midst of the recession: "Let's step out of the usual boundaries of analysis of our current economic crisis and ask a radical question—What if the crisis of 2008 represents something much more fundamental than a deep recession? What if it is telling us that the whole growth model created over the last 50 years is simply unsustainable economically and ecologically and that 2008 was when we hit the wall—when Mother Nature and the market both said no more."[10]

We can't know just how much of a role such ideological blindness played in this particular event. It is possible that what occurred is largely explainable by natural fluctuations, new global realities, simple greed, and poor decisions. But in the long term, if Cultural Maturity's picture holds, the implications of this kind of analysis will be increasingly important to consider. Economic structures that can serve us—structures that can support advancement and be stable and sustainable—must be maturely systemic. And they must be so not just in their appreciation of technical complexities, but also in reflecting a more complete picture of how economies—and people—ultimately work.[11]

---

10 Friedman, Thomas, New York Times, February 2009

11 With my reflections on government, I've listed several attributes we might predictably find with a next chapter in its evolution. These economics-related observations suggest one more—a new, more mature, limits-acknowledging relationship between government and the economic sphere. Representative government today not only fails to be one-person-one-vote in any Whole-Person sense, much of the time it fails to represent people at all. More accurately it represents wealth. Someone—and usually that means a large corporation—can get as much representation as they can buy. This really can't continue to work going forward.

Going Too Far

Before we turn to Chapter Six's more specifically theoretical reflections, I'm going to throw in one additional Creative Systems concept. It provocatively describes a critical dynamic common in our time. Creative Systems Theory calls this dynamic *Transitional Absurdity*. The kind of ideological blindness in the economic sphere I just described provides one example. But there are many others.

It is hard to ignore that much that we witness today seems not at all sane. And we must not ignore it—we pay a high price for denial. But it turns out that many phenomena particular to our time that may appear ludicrous, if not disastrous in their implications, are predicted by culture's developmental mechanisms. Some are simple reactions to limits we would prefer to deny, or to complexities that stretch us beyond what we are yet able to tolerate. But many relate more directly to the Dilemma of Trajectory.

It is beyond our scope in this book to delve deeply into the mechanisms that underlie particular Transitional Absurdities. But as a general principle, Transitional Absurdities reflect dynamics in which cultural evolution's trajectory to this point is taken sufficiently far beyond its usefulness that we become distanced from critical aspects of who we are and what matters to us. We encounter Modern Age realities extended well beyond their timeliness and as well as postmodern sensibilities that have long since stopped being of value. One result is that we begin to act in ways that are hard to describe as anything but bizarre. At the least, we find ourselves without the ability to choose in any purposeful way.

As a start, I would include on my list (though there are many more examples):

■ The unending triviality of mass material culture. (Human value becomes increasingly tied more to empty consumption than to significance.)

■ Our truly amazing capacity to ignore damage done to the earth's environment and to deny potential ecological catastrophes. (Our ability to hide from the obvious when it comes to nature is remarkable.)

■ The previously noted superficial pettiness that defines much of modern politics and our bewildering willingness to accept it as leadership. (So often the important questions are not even voiced, much less usefully addressed—this in the face of leadership challenges that could not be more immense or pressing.)

■ The common belief in certain circles that new technologies alone can solve all of the world's problems. (At the very least, this belief requires that we ignore the obvious fact that the ability to invent and the capacity to use invention wisely are not at all the same thing.)

■ And at a more individual scale, today's obsession with the most superficial aspects of physical appearance (witness our current infatuation with plastic surgery), rampant obesity (and eating disorders more generally), widespread drug abuse (illegal and prescription), and the use of sex to sell most every kind of product. (I grieve that we can be so alienated from our own bodies.)

I made brief reference to the most dangerous of Transitional Absurdities in speaking of the two-edged–sword potential of emerging information technologies. In our time, we are particularly vulnerable to confusing artificial stimulation with substance. Addictive artificial substitutes for significance are not limited to the world of new media. We see this dynamic in more everyday forms with "if it bleeds, it leads" journalism and with movies and television programming that reduce to little more than shootings, car crashes, and flashes of erotic titillation. When we confuse artificial stimulation with substance, we not only leave ourselves without guidance and real fulfillment, we do damage to the internal sensibilities needed to effectively discern where meaning lies.

The concept of Transitional Absurdity adds important further insight into the phenomenon I've referred to as our time's "crisis of purpose." Remember my conversation with Alex at the book's beginning. I think of the depth of dissociation Alex felt from himself and the world around him as a generalized expression of Transitional Absurdity. The "theater of the absurd" of Camus or Kafka makes a good reference. In part what these artistic works describe is simply today's loss of familiar cultural sureties and the frightening possibility that there is nothing to replace them—and I'm sure these factors played into what Alex felt. But these works are also about fearing a fundamental disconnect from anything that might matter. I'm reminded of the hero, Meursault, in Camus' *The Stranger* turning to find nothing but "the benign indifference of the universe."[12]

In other writings, I describe additional Transitional Absurdities and clarify how those listed here reflect the kind of "overshooting-the-mark" dynamics I have noted.[13] For our purposes, the notion helps make phenomena we see today more understandable. It also provides an ironic further kind of hope. It supports the conclusion that much that might seem most indicative of a calamitous future is in fact predicted by how human change processes inherently work. The concept of Transitional Absurdity makes clear that we can't stop with current circumstances. But Cultural Maturity's more systemic narrative also affirms that there is no reason—other than a lack of courage—that we should.

In our time, we witness, simultaneously, new contributions that are profound in their implications and an unsettling array of beliefs and actions that can seem quite crazy. It is essential that we not lose sight of the former. And if we are not to succumb to cynicism, it is also important that we understand much of that craziness for what it is: not some sign of the end of things, but the result of old realities taken to the point of absurdity. The book's next chapter will help make more clear how, with each of the absurdities I have listed, Cultural Maturity's "new common sense" provides a solution and a creative way forward.

A quick summary:

As culture's past parental function ceases to be a defining force, we become newly responsible for the truths that cultural guideposts

---

12 Camus, Albert (translated by Mathew Ward), *The Stranger*, Random House, New York, 1989

13 See, in particular, *Cultural Maturity: A Guidebook for the Future*.

previously provided. This new responsibility requires both being more conscious when making choices and reaching more deeply into our natures as complex beings when determining what, for us, is true. In the process, conclusions of all sorts change fundamentally, from the most personal of preferences to how we conceive of our institutions to our ideas about human advancement. The changes in ourselves that make all this possible are of a different, more specifically integrative sort than we have seen with previous major cultural change points. One result is a depth and systemic sophistication of understanding that before now would have made no sense, and which previously would not have been an option.

CHAPTER 6

Theoretical Perspective—
A Closer Look at the Concept
of Cultural Maturity

Creativity is the universal of universals.
— Alfred North Whitehead

A few questions:

1. What exactly do I mean when I say that Cultural Maturity's changes are developmentally predicted?
2. What are the cognitive mechanisms that underlie Cultural Maturity's changes?
3. How do we best understand the changes that Cultural Maturity's cognitive reordering produce and their pertinence to the human challenges ahead?

While Cultural Maturity's changes can seem almost self-evident when we are familiar with them, at first they can be tricky to fully make sense of. Some of this trickiness is inherent in any developmental reordering. I've made reference to how developmental changes present a chicken-and-egg conundrum—before we've experienced them first hand, it can be difficult to get our minds around where they take us. But with Cultural Maturity's changes, we also confront the new cognitive orientation that defines experience once we've stepped over Cultural Maturity's threshold. Cultural Maturity's whole-box-of-crayons systemic picture stretches understanding in particularly fundamental ways.

My hope with this chapter is to make what Cultural Maturity involves as conceptually solid as I can given the constraints of time and space that come with an introductory book. I will address earlier key conceptual notions with greater detail. I will also attempt to make the various aspects of the argument that I have presented for Cultural Maturity and its necessity as much as possible a single argument.

These more specifically conceptual reflections will often require covering complex notions in a lickety-split fashion. People whose primary interest lies with the basic idea of Cultural Maturity and how it applies to good decision-making may find parts of this chapter providing more theory than they have interest in. But for those who wish to have a solid conceptual understanding of Cultural Maturity's changes and what produces them, these further observations fill out previous reflections in important ways.

Earlier chapters have set the stage for these more conceptual observations. In Chapter One, I described how we can think of Cultural Maturity as providing a necessary greater sophistication in how we humans think and act—an essential "growing up" as a species. With the last four chapters, we've explored this result by examining the way in which important challenges before us as a species require new kinds of human capacities. I've described how the concept of Cultural Maturity can help us understand why new human capacities are needed, tease apart what such new capacities involve, and make sense of how we might realize them.

I will start here with a more detailed look at the analogy between personal maturity and Cultural Maturity that gives the concept of Cultural Maturity its name. These reflections will help make fuller sense of why Cultural Maturity's changes produce the kinds of new capacities that they do. They will also provide additional support for my claim that something like what the concept of Cultural Maturity describes is really the only option going forward.

I will then turn to the cognitive processes that produce Cultural Maturity's changes and more specifically address how this cognitive reordering alters not just *what* we think, but also *how* we think. I will also make more explicit how the more encompassing and complete kind of understanding needed to address today's new questions is a natural outcome of these cognitive changes.

Next I will return to a now-familiar way of speaking of the kind of understanding that results: Culturally mature perspective is more explicitly systemic. I've proposed that culturally mature perspective requires not just that we think systemically in the sense of including pertinent parts, but that we do so in new, more dynamic and sophisticated ways. We will look more specifically at this assertion and some of its implications for understanding in the future.

Then—briefly—I will touch on the particular conceptual approach used by Creative Systems Theory and how it lets us develop needed new-truth concepts. I will draw on two now-familiar themes—the role of polarity in understanding and the fact that intelligence has multiple aspects—to examine how a creative frame offers an effective way to make the conceptual leap required to think with the needed new systemic sophistication.

I will conclude by turning to the developmental sort of evolutionary perspective that gives us the concept of Cultural Maturity. I will briefly address what makes this general kind of idea new. I will also describe how understanding what makes it new helps us separate the wheat from the chaff in our thinking about the future—tease apart different ways of thinking about the tasks ahead and discern those that can be most useful.

Throughout this chapter, I will give particular attention to how Cultural Maturity's changes are different from what we have known, not just in their particulars, but in the kind of change they represent. This fundamental sort of difference has been at least implied with each previous chapter, but fully grasping the concept of Cultural Maturity and its implications depends on understanding it with some depth. While this particular focus will add to the demands of this chapter, it will also make the insights this chapter provides particularly significant. The ability of the concept of Cultural Maturity to provide guidance going forward hinges on this fundamental difference.

Personal and Cultural Maturity

Reflecting more deeply on the developmental analogy between personal maturity and the developmental demands of our time helps make the concept of Cultural Maturity more concrete. It also more solidly establishes the very particular nature of Cultural Maturity's changes.

Creative Systems Theory proposes, as I've noted, that related changes in a similar way fundamentally reorder experience in the mature stages of human change processes wherever we find them. But for this inquiry, it continues to be sufficient that we focus on the basic analogy. With each of the new capacities we've examined over the previous four chapters, I've observed that we find more limited versions with the shift that produces maturity in our individual lifetimes.

I've emphasized that the word "maturity" as we apply it to personal development has two meanings with very different developmental implications. This distinction should now be clear. But because each meaning has its appropriate historical associations and has lessons to teach, giving it more specific attention makes a good place to start.

The first and more familiar meaning of maturity relates to the transition through which adolescents become adults. Maturity in this first sense is about assuming adult responsibility and adult authority (and leaving behind adolescent ways). It describes coming to live independent lives, finding professions, perhaps having children.

When people speak casually of a need to "grow up" in our human behavior, they often make implied analogy with this first definition. But while this first meaning has useful associations, the correct historical parallel is not with today. Rather, it is with the advent of culture's Modern Age (seen in the West from the Renaissance into the twentieth century). "Growing up" in this sense culturally gave us democratic rule, scientific objectivity, and modern institutional forms.

In contrast, as I've described, Cultural Maturity finds its parallel with the developmental tasks of life's second half. The changes that produce this second, "more mature" kind of maturity in individual development tend to become most apparent as we approach midlife, though sometimes we see earlier intimations. Related shifts are common, for example, in people confronting death or serious illness. But midlife provides the most ready reference.

Making analogy with this second sort of maturity can seem less clear-cut if for no other reason than that most of the related cultural tasks still lie before us.[1] But once understood, our second definition

---

1   There is also the fact that today, in contrast to earlier times in culture, we tend not to acknowledge and respect the developmental challenges of life's

provides the necessary associations—and needed guidance. We find direct parallels with each of Cultural Maturity's main characteristics in the essential demands—and achievements—of second-half-of-life maturity in our personal human development.

Certainly we find parallels in changes that pertain to our relationship with parents, both real and internalized. I've described how Cultural Maturity requires that we step beyond perceiving culture as a mythic parent. Personal maturity involves a related shift in our relationship to our biological parents. With the heroic maturity of young adulthood, we leave our parents physically. Midlife challenges us to leave our biological parents in a more ultimate way—to let go of them as symbols. To move forward, we must step beyond viewing our parents either as more than human (using our images of them to create illusions of safety and specialness) or as less so (making them excuses for our failures). If we are successful in confronting the developmental tasks of midlife, this is when we first truly leave our parents. Importantly, it is also the time when we really first meet them—simply as people.

Personal second-half-of life maturity also involves confronting new developmental challenges. In previous chapters, I've introduced the way in which many of these challenges—and the new capacities that result from successfully engaging them—find direct parallels in challenges and changes we confront today at a cultural level. Midlife is a time for recognizing personal bigotries and knee-jerk assumptions that may have before gotten in the way of our maturely seeing the world around us (our more private "ideologies"). It is a time for acknowledging limits, for grappling in new ways with what may and may not be possible, and also for confronting the fact of our mortality (life's ultimate limit—both to what we can do and what we can know). It is a time for addressing the often-confusing complexities, ambiguities, and paradoxes inherent in both relationships and personal identity—and

---

later years. We are more likely to associate second-half-of-life changes with being "over the hill" than with new developmental challenges and new learnings that, if successfully engaged, can make people in their later years appropriately venerated. Creative Systems Theory describes how these differing views of life's second half are developmentally predicted. (See *Cultural Maturity: A Guidebook for the Future*.)

learning to hold both relationships and identity in fuller ways. It is also a time for stepping back and reflecting on what is ultimately important to us, for reexamining old goals (our personal notions of "progress"), and asking afresh what will make our choices most life-affirming.

Along with providing associations that help us delineate the general characteristics of Cultural Maturity's changes, the developmental analogy also brings attention to the uniqueness of these changes. With both second-half-of-life personal maturity and Cultural Maturity we confront not just specific new developmental challenges, but also a whole new relationship to existence as an endeavor. The recognition that we confront a completely different kind of developmental task—indeed, a wholly different orientation to life's tasks—with second-half-of-life personal maturity is a key part of what makes the analogy with personal maturity so helpful for understanding today's cultural changes.

The specific way I used the word "responsibility" in the previous chapter highlights this sense in which in both instances we are dealing with something fully new. I proposed that culturally mature responsibility is necessarily a double responsibility—we become responsible not just for making good choices, but also for determining what makes something a good choice.

Responsibility in young adulthood is of the more familiar, basic kind. It is about gaining knowledge and about establishing one's place in the world—in work, in love. It is the responsibility of being accountable for one's actions and being willing to shoulder one's load, the responsibility of being a good person and doing good work. Such responsibility asks a lot of us, but it does so within the familiar guidelines of family expectations and the personal beliefs we've brought to addressing the heroic[2] challenges of life's first half.

Responsibility in life's second half, to the degree that we are willing to take on the requisite developmental challenges, is of that wholly different, double sort. It requires that we both question old truths and get more deeply at what for us makes something true. As with culturally mature responsibility, the needed new responsibility is not just

---

2 It might be better to again say "heroic/romantic." As with culture, the stories we tell about life's first half can reflect either of these complementary, polarity-permeated sorts of narratives, applied alone or in combination.

responsibility for doing what we're supposed to do—or even acting intelligently. It is responsibility for thinking with new depth about what ultimately matters and, whenever possible, acting wisely.

Parallels that shed additional light on the Dilemma of Trajectory help further fill out both what Cultural Maturity asks of us and how its changes are of a new sort. I've described how culture's story up to this point has followed a generally consistent "onward-and-upward" course toward ever-increasing individuality, authority over the world around us, and technical achievement. And I've proposed that there is an important structural sense in which going forward as we have is no longer an option.

Personal development includes dynamics that present us with something very similar to culture's Dilemma of Trajectory. The first half of personal development follows a related onward-and-upward course, one that is marked in a parallel way by processes that produce increasing individuality, authority over the world around us, and through the skills we learn, technical prowess. And as we see with culture's trajectory in our time, with the second half of personal development this general direction of change, in isolation, stops being sufficient. If we continue on as we have, the second half of life becomes increasingly troubled, at best a thin caricature of youth. Indeed, we often find thoughts and actions very similar to those I've referred to as Transitional Absurdities. (Think of the absurd behaviors that can come with a "midlife crisis."[3])

The developmental analogy also supports the conclusion that the Dilemma of Trajectory need not be the end of us—and affirms the nature of the needed way forward. Personal maturity's changes, in a more limited but related way to what we see with the changes of Cultural Maturity, are integrative and systemic. When we are struck by the particular sophistication and integrity of someone who has lived his or her later years well, it is these more integrative second-half achievements we are recognizing. At a personal scale, individuality, authority, and technical prowess each derive more systemic definitions.

We can take these themes one at a time. With personal maturity, individuality, in fact, continues to grow, often manifesting in particu-

---

3 Midlife crises tend to similarly involve "overshooting the mark." When we engage second-half-of-life developmental tasks in a timely fashion, midlife transitions most often play out relatively smoothly.

larly powerful and delightfully idiosyncratic ways. We more comfort-
ably embrace what most authentically makes us who we are. But, as
part of this if we successfully take on the tasks of second-half-of-life
development, the tendency toward difference that underlies how before we have thought about individuality becomes counterbalanced
by an equally important, greater appreciation for connectedness.[4]

With authority we see similar, more integrative changes. Second-
half-of-life developmental tasks challenge us to take ultimate leadership and responsibility in our lives. But personal maturity's changes
also mean that we better bring the whole of ourselves to our determinations. The result—similar to what we see with Cultural Maturity but
on a smaller scale—is an at once more effective and more humble kind
of authority. We see authority that better embraces life's big picture,
including its uncertainties and demanding complexities.

And we also encounter something similar when it comes to new
skills and technical abilities. While second-half-of-life changes make
us capable of much more, they also bring new perspective with regard
to where new skills and abilities can help us and where they cannot.
We become more conscious of our limits and more wise in how we apply what we are capable of doing.

The analogy with second-half-of-life personal maturity also
helps us in a final important way that we will later return to when
addressing the future of hope. It supports the particular richness of
Cultural Maturity as an accomplishment. Second-half-of-life personal maturity produces an essential filling out of experience. If we
take care with language, we could apply a word I've often used here
and say that taking on the challenges of midlife marks the beginning of a "completeness" in who we are that has not before been
possible. Again, I don't mean "complete" in the sense of being fin-

---

4 The Myth of the Individual applies in a more limited sense to the changes
   of personal development. We've seen how individuality as we tend to think
   of it embraces at best half of what it means to be a whole person. We've
   also seen how, when we take such a partial and limited definition beyond
   its timeliness, it stops providing a felt sense of identity. With wisdom in personal development, we better recognize the importance of connectedness.
   We also more deeply appreciate what makes us particular, authentically
   who we are.

ished. The developmental challenges of personal maturity extend through the whole of the second half of life—and even then, what we are able to understand is far from complete. But personal maturity *is* about completeness in the sense of learning to draw more fully and consciously on the whole of what makes us who we are. In a related way, Cultural Maturity, in helping us draw more fully and consciously on what makes us human, is an expression not just of something positive, but of something with profound and even ultimate significance.[5]

Cultural Maturity's Cognitive Reordering

To make full sense of Cultural Maturity's changes, we need to give some focused attention to the cognitive processes that produce them. Understanding how Cultural Maturity's cognitive reordering works helps further clarify how Cultural Maturity's changes result in the new kinds of capacities we've looked at. It also provides important insight into the new ways of thinking that will be increasingly required by the challenges ahead—into both what makes the more dynamic and complete truth concepts that we need possible, and also what ultimately defines them.

History helps put these changes in perspective. Cultural Maturity's cognitive reordering is new—fundamentally so—but each new chapter in culture's evolving story has similarly been marked by organizational leaps. The leap that brought us Modern Age thought provides the most pertinent comparison. The new sensibilities introduced with the fresh artistic visions of Michelangelo and Leonardo da Vinci in the fifteenth century—and that were later filled out with the seventeenth-century conceptual formulations of Newton and Descartes—did more than just alter our conclusions. They reflected a whole new kind of understanding—indeed, a new type of conceptual organization.

---

5 While the analogy with personal maturity provides important insight, personal maturity and Cultural Maturity also have key differences and we can get into trouble in our thinking if we don't recognize them. *Cultural Maturity: A Guidebook for the Future* teases apart the most important of these differences.

We can summarize what then became different with the simple observation that these changes resulted in a new, from-a-balcony kind of perspective—what we commonly refer to when we use the word "objective." Everything we commonly identify with Modern Age advancement—the rise of individualism, more democratic governmental forms, the Industrial Revolution, scientific preeminence, and a more personal conception of the divine—can be understood to follow from this basic cognitive reorganization and the new kind of perspective it produced.

In a similar way, we can make sense of everything about culturally mature understanding—what it asks of us, why it does so, and why we might expect the specific changes it describes—in terms of changes in the mechanisms through which we make sense of ourselves and the world around us. The cognitive reorganization that happens at Cultural Maturity's threshold is related, but also new in basic ways.

Cultural Maturity's cognitive reordering involves two complementary processes. The previous chapter's look at the double responsibility that is required for a culturally mature relationship with truth hinted at how these two processes work together to produce culturally mature perspective. The first process involves a more complete kind of stepping back. The second process gives us the new depth of engagement needed if the result is to be not just broader perspective, but the deeply embodied kind of understanding that mature—wise—decision-making requires.[6]

With the first kind of process, what we step back from has multiple aspects. Most immediately, we step back from ourselves as cultural beings. As we do, we become newly able to recognize culture's previous mythologized, "parental" status, and to begin moving beyond it. But we also step back from internal aspects of ourselves in ways that were not possible before. I've emphasized the importance of being newly conscious of parts of ourselves that before were projected. Doing so requires this new kind of stepping back. I've also described the new ability to step back from the whole of intelligence that comes with Cultural Maturity's changes. In the end, we more fully step back from the whole of our internal complexity.

6 We see more limited versions of each of these cognitive processes with the changes of personal maturity we just looked at.

The particular way our relationship with our multiple intelligences changes with this stepping-back process helps distinguish what we see from what has taken place at previous major cultural change points. Stepping back from more familiar ways of knowing played a similarly central role, for example, in the Enlightenment's cognitive reorganization. Modern Age perspective distanced us from the more mystical sensibilities that had permeated the beliefs of the Middle Ages.

But what we saw then was different in key ways from what we see with Cultural Maturity's stepping back. This distancing was achieved by a polar separating of the rational from more non-rational aspects of experience. It also involved allying conscious awareness specifically with rationality. Modern Age truth's from-a-balcony sense of final clarity was achieved by separating experience into polar opposite "objective" and "subjective" worlds.

The first part of Cultural Maturity's cognitive reordering continues this stepping-back process. In an important sense, it also completes it. Awareness comes to stand separate from the whole of our intelligence's systemic complexity—including the rational. In doing so, it takes us beyond the identification with particular intelligences that has been a characteristic of previous cultural stages. It also takes us beyond polarity. Culturally mature perspective steps back equally from sensibilities we've before thought of as subjective and from ways of thinking that we've before identified with objectivity.

This first part of Cultural Maturity's cognitive reordering effectively moves us beyond the most obvious of past ideological beliefs, but by itself, it cannot be enough. And at some level we know this. While the more complete stepping back can at first feel exhilarating, it can also feel precarious—stepping back this fully can leave us feeling strangely distanced from ourselves. It is here that we experience the Transitional dynamics that produce both postmodern "anything-goes" sensibilities and Transitional Absurdities. We need the second kind of process if our thinking is to again have coherence and provide useful direction.

The second part of Cultural Maturity's cognitive reordering produces Cultural Maturity's specifically integrative outcome. The kind of process it involves is not just different from what we have known before; it finds no parallel at all in previous cultural change points. Along with more fully stepping back from the multiple aspects of our human complexity, Cultural Maturity's cognitive changes also involve more directly engaging that complexity. We plumb experience with a fundamentally new kind of depth. In the process, we come to more consciously and fully embody all that makes us who we are. This second kind of dynamic is essential to culturally mature understanding, both the ability to get more directly at significance and the possibility of thinking in new, more nuanced and complete ways.

Once again, while diverse aspects of our human complexity are involved, for the purposes of this inquiry, it works to keep things simple and focus on intelligence. I've described how culturally mature understanding requires the conscious application of multiple aspects of intelligence—more of our diverse ways of knowing. It requires thinking in a rational sense—indeed, it expands rationality's role—but equally it requires that we more directly apply the more feeling, imagining, and sensing aspects of who we are. With the second part of Cultural Maturity's cognitive reordering, we more deeply engage the whole of intelligence—and by virtue of this, in the end, the whole of ourselves. With this, culturally mature perspective becomes more integrative both in the sense of helping us reconnect with aspects of experience we've previously distanced ourselves from, and also in the sense of helping us understand in more complete ways whatever our concern may be.[7]

Both halves of this two-part cognitive process—both the more complete stepping back and the new depth of engagement—are needed for culturally mature perspective. Put in the language of systems, systemic perspective of a culturally mature sort requires that we both more consciously acknowledge and more directly draw on the whole of ourselves as systems. The diagram in Figure 6-1 depicts this dual process. Creative Systems Theory calls the result *Integrative Meta-perspective*. The term is a mouthful, but it quite precisely describes what we see.

---

7 When previously I observed that culturally mature perspective involves stepping back from ways of understanding that before we might have treated as objective, as well as those that we've thought of as subjective, a person could have appropriately protested that much of philosophy has been about doing just that. The difference is that we have not before in the same sense been able to step back from the "objective" as one aspect of this more nuanced and integrated picture of understanding.

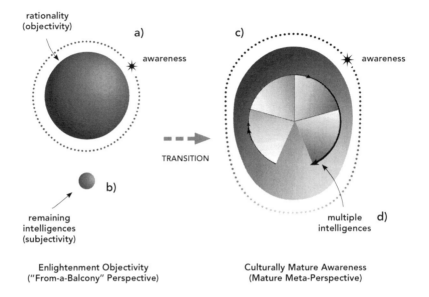

Enlightenment Objectivity   Culturally Mature Awareness
("From-a-Balcony" Perspective)   (Mature Meta-Perspective)

a) Rational intelligence (allied with awareness to produce from-a-balcony objectivity)

b) The subjective (all remaining intelligences as experienced in Modern Age reality)

c) < --------- * --------- > Culturally mature awareness in its various more and less conscious permutations[8]

d) Multiple intelligences (made newly explicit with culturally mature perspective)

Fig. 6-1. Cultural Maturity's Cognitive Reordering[9]

The two notions that I've used to introduce the specific kind of systemic understanding that comes with culturally mature perspective—the "bridging" of traditional polarities at Cultural Maturity's

---

8   Earlier I observed how being maturely conscious is not the same as being conscious of everything. I also noted that different intelligences require different degrees of conscious involvement.

9   The relationship of poles on the left side of the diagram reflects what we see with Modern Age dynamics--see Fig.6-4. (See www.CSTHome.org for a more detailed look at this diagram.)

threshold and the box of crayons image—each reflect natural outcomes of this dual process. Culturally mature perspective lets us better step back from and recognize polarities (those that relate to intelligence's aspects, such as facts and feelings, and also polarity more generally). It also lets us more effectively get our minds around polar relationships with the result that polarities can now be systemically "bridged." In a similar way, Cultural Maturity's cognitive changes make possible whole-box-of-crayons perspective. We become newly able to step back and recognize the rich multiplicity that underlies human understanding (intelligence's multiplicity, but also our multifaceted natures more broadly). And we become able both to more deeply access this complexity of hues and to draw on its various aspects in the most creative ways. With time, Cultural Maturity's cognitive changes make whole-box-of-crayons perspective seem like common sense.

We can also understand each of the new human capacities I focused on in the previous four chapters in terms of these cognitive changes. With regard to re-owning denigrated aspects of ourselves, Cultural Maturity's cognitive reordering helps us better recognize projection and see beyond ideological easy answers with their "single-crayon" conclusions. In doing so, it helps us appreciate a more sophisticated and complete picture of whatever our concern may be.

With regard to more effectively addressing limits, these same changes let us more readily acknowledge and tolerate real contraints. I've described how systemically partial views, by their nature, hide myths of limitlessness. Cultural Maturity's whole-box-of-crayons perspective makes real limits more easily recognized and appreciated as intrinsic to how things work.

With regard to idealizations that have protected us from the full demands of relationships and identity, Cultural Maturity's cognitive changes reveal a larger and more complex, but also ultimately more rewarding picture. As we better appreciate how every person "contains multitudes," we engage human interconnections of every sort in ways that more accurately perceive the other. We are also able to more fully embrace our own personal richness and complexity.

With regard to reconceiving the bottom-line values and truths we use to make our choices, these same changes let us think about what matters in new, more encompassing ways. Whatever the context, whether our interest is more personal or more encompassing, these changes make it possible to get at what matters with a depth and completeness that was not possible before now.

Appreciating the way Cultural Maturity's cognitive reordering works also further clarifies how the Dilemma of Trajectory need not be the end of us. Understanding—and understanding the future—becomes about giving more full and complete expression to all that makes us who we are. We no longer need to fear estrangement from important aspects of what makes us human. The more integrative picture that comes with Cultural Maturity's cognitive reordering reconciles what otherwise would be a dead-end circumstance.

I've previously suggested a further important conceptual consequence of this new, more consciously encompassing picture. It concerns how we use the word "objective" and should now make fuller sense. Enlightenment thought claimed ultimate objectivity, but as should now be clear, this was, in fact, objectivity of a most preliminary and limited sort. Besides leaving culture's parental status untouched, it left experience as a whole divided—objective (in the old sense) opposed to subjective, mind opposed to body, thoughts opposed to feelings (and anything else that does not conform to modernity's rationalist/materialist worldview). In one sense, culturally mature perspective is less "objective" than what it replaces—being that it draws on aspects of intelligence that before gave us the more subjective parts of experience. But while culturally mature perspective produces less once-and-for-all kinds of truth than we have been accustomed to, it is ultimately *more* objective—if by "objective" we mean better able to grasp all that is involved. We cannot ultimately claim to be objective if we have left out half of the evidence.

Rethinking Systems

I've drawn repeatedly on the language of systems and suggested that it provides a particularly useful way to talk about the kind of understanding needed to address future challenges. In doing so, I've emphasized that culturally mature understanding requires that we think systemically in some fundamentally new ways.

The previous section's reflections on Cultural Maturity's cognitive reordering provide insight into this essential assertion. They help clarify how the needed more dynamic and encompassing kind of systemic understanding reflects more than just some technical advance in our thinking. We see how the needed new systemic sophistication is a product not just of getting smarter, but of culturally mature perspective's more conscious and encompassing vantage point for making sense of the world. These reflections also help us better appreciate what makes the needed more sophisticated kind of systemic understanding increasingly an option. Not only does Integrative Meta-perspective make more sophisticated systemic thinking possible, anytime we effectively apply such perspective, at least in some informal way, we draw on this more complete kind of systemic understanding.

With this section's more specific reflections on systemic understanding, we look a bit more closely at just what is new. I've described how we need to take a couple of new steps in our thinking. First, we need to think systemically in ways that better reflect the fact that we are alive. We also need to think in ways that more effectively reflect the particular sort of life that makes us human. We've made a good start with understanding both of these steps, but a quick, more focused examination helps us avoid common traps in our thinking. It also serves to set the stage for later, more detailed reflections on the whole-box-of-crayons kind of systemic discernments that the future will increasingly require—including the kind on which this book's developmental argument is based.

Appreciating the importance of thinking systemically in ways that better reflect that we are living beings begins with the recognition that our systemic models have, until quite recently, most always been mechanical models. They may acknowledge intricacies and complex interconnections, and even the role of uncertainty.[10] But even when the system is a human body or an ecosystem teeming with organisms, the language most often has remained that of a good engineer—hydraulics and forces, actions and their concomitant reactions. While before now this shortcoming hasn't been a

---

10 For example, if we add chaos theory to more conventional mechanistic formulations, uncertainty becomes specifically acknowledged But while such results are expressly non-deterministic, they remain mechanistic.

huge obstacle, we are not machines—we are living systems. In our time, ignoring this fact increasingly creates problems.[11]

A basic question helps get at this first part of the new systemic task more conceptually: How do we think about difference if our ideas are to honor the fact that we are alive? Besides helping us appreciate what makes needed new systemic ideas fundamentally new, attempting to answer this question also highlights the multiple ways in which systemic thinking can go astray. Systemic understanding is unusual for the diverse—even opposite—worldviews it can be used to justify.

Efforts to answer this question confront us with what Creative Systems Theory calls the *Dilemma of Differentiation*. The simple fact that culturally mature truth requires that we make distinctions immediately puts us in a pickle. Differentiation—the ability to say "this as opposed to that"—is ultimately what makes thinking work. But usual ways of addressing difference leave us short of the required dynamism.

We can miss the mark in two opposite ways when addressing difference. We encounter both kinds of traps with advocates of systemic thought. The most obvious kind of trap is the one previously noted. Thinkers depict difference in traditional "parts" terms—that is, in a gears-and-pulleys, mechanistic manner. Such thinking alone cannot help us today. No matter how subtle and sensitive our delineations, when we put the parts together, we end up back in a machine world.

Less often we encounter an opposite, yet just as deadly kind of trap. Popular writers who use systems language—particularly writers of a more humanist or spiritual bent—may largely ignore parts and focus only on relationship. Very often the result is ideas that are ultimately elaborate ways of saying "all is one." Recognizing connectedness can be comforting, and doing so identifies a truth that is just as important and as accurate as the "all is many" claims of atomistic or mechanistic belief. But ignoring the importance of parts makes for impoverished conception

---

11 The importance of finding ways to think about living systems that reflect that they are alive was appreciated early on in the evolution of systems thinking. For example, this was one of the recognitions that first inspired Ludwig von Bertalanffy to develop his groundbreaking General Systems Theory early in the previous century. But formulations able to bring meaningful detail to such thinking have been slow in coming.

at best. Worse, it makes for misleading conception. Real relationship (oneness in the systemic sense we have interest in)—whether personal or conceptual—requires difference. Certainly life does.[12]

The important recognition for our task is that Cultural Maturity's cognitive changes inherently produce a third, more dynamic kind of systemic understanding. Integrative Meta-perspective gives us not just different conclusions, but a fully different way of seeing the world. When viewed from this more encompassing perspective, the two alternative kinds of "systemic" interpretations I've described reveal themselves to be opposite, systemically partial—in the end, ideological—positions. I've emphasized the fact that Integrative Meta-perspective increases our appreciation for both relatedness and difference.[13] In doing so, it not only fundamentally challenges each of these more limited interpretations; it beats each of them at their own game.

One of the most important results of this more complete way of seeing things is that it makes it possible to address living systems in more life-acknowledging terms. The recognition that culturally mature perspective "bridges" conceptual polarities more generally reflects this increasingly essential result. When we "bridge" any polarity and really do it (instead of just adding, averaging, or merging polarity's opposites), we are thrust into a wholly different, more dynamic and encompassing kind of reality.[14]

---

12 Connectedness-celebrating formulations in the end give us nothing new. I've described how the Modern Age narrative juxtaposed a heroic definition of significance with a more romantic countervailing impulse. Such formulations are most often just new expressions of this polar-opposite impulse.

13 Earlier I made reference to how we see this result—increased appreciation for both relatedness and difference—whenever we reincorporate projections. We see it equally when we leave behind demonized projections (for example, with bigotry) and when we get beyond more idealized projections (for example, with love). In the end, we see it with culturally mature understanding of every sort.

14 To fully appreciate how the "bridging" of polarities applies to the thinking-of-life-in-living-terms conundrum, we need to recognize how, in modern times, aspects of polarity have often been hidden. In our more distant history, life was described explicitly in terms of polarity—think of Aristotle's

The Dilemma of Differentiation pertains most obviously to living systems, but it also has broader implications. Cultural Maturity's cognitive changes help us understand any kind of system that ultimately defies mechanistic conception in more dynamic terms. Increasingly, the best of thinking about purely physical systems at least stretches the boundaries of mechanistic formulations. For example, it may observe how simple physical processes can be "emergent" or "self-organizing," suggesting a more dynamic, even generative picture. I've noted how modern physics "bridges" polarities at every turn—matter with energy, time with space, observer with observed, certainty with uncertainty. Existence as a whole becomes a fundamentally more dynamic enterprise when seen through a culturally mature lens.[15]

The basic recognition that today's challenges require thinking that does a better job of addressing living systems takes us a long way toward capturing the kind of understanding the future requires, but if our concern is ourselves, we also need the additional step I've mentioned. We need to think in ways that reflect not just life's generative dynamism, but also that we are dynamic and alive in the particular ways that make us human. This critique of systemic perspectives—in particular how it has placed what is necessarily new in a historical context—reflects this essential further step. This step, too, comes part and parcel with Cultural Maturity's cognitive changes.

I've described how Cultural Maturity's cognitive reordering involves both more fully stepping back from and more deeply engaging our various internal aspects (for example, intelligence's multiplicity). I've also described how the box-of-crayons image reflects where these changes

---

"unmoved mover," or Henri Bergson's "élan vital," each juxtaposed with the structures of animate form. Mechanistic science has chosen to dismiss one pole and make it all gears-and-pulleys anatomy and physiology (with more difficult to describe observations reduced to "epiphenomena" within this basic engineering-model explanation).

15 In recognizing this common systemic dynamism, it is important that we don't just lump the non-living, the simply biological, and the human together. Popular writers of a more spiritual bent can make the universe as a whole "alive" in a way that may seem inspiring, but which is ultimately trivial.

take us. Systemic understanding that reflects our "I contain multitudes" complex human natures is the result.

This additional step in our thinking is essential if our ideas are to effectively address human concerns such as the challenges we've touched on in previous chapters. These have been not just specifically human challenges, but also challenges that specifically require that we get beyond single-crayon ideological assumptions. This further, whole-box-of-crayons step also has major significance for the tasks ahead because it contains the insights we need to develop detailed, culturally mature conceptual frameworks, whether our interest lies with ourselves or with how our ideas about the world around us have been different at different times and places.

In Chapter Five, I observed how effectively addressing human concerns in times ahead will require two kinds of new systemic truth notions: concepts that reflect the encompassing whole of what makes something true, and concepts that can help us discern and articulate detailed, context-specific kinds of truth. I described how we can think of the first kind of truth concept—the kind that I applied when I proposed that moral decision-making is ultimately about deciding what choice is most "life-affirming"[16]—as "whole-box" systemic truth. And I described how we can think of truth concepts that help us make detailed and contextually specific kinds of discernments as "crayon-specific" systemic truths. They give primary attention to particular hues (while not forgetting the box[17]). Each of these represents a kind of distinction that only becomes possible with Integrative Meta-perspective and the more complete kind of systemic understanding that results.[18]

To summarize the systemic challenge: We need to learn to think about systems of all sorts in more dynamic and complete ways. This is particularly the case when our concern is living systems. We also need to learn to think

---

16 More precisely, I could have said "human life–affirming."

17 When we forget the box, we end up making a single crayon the truth. The result is ideology.

18 Notice that the whole-box-of-crayons picture, like the "bridging" of polarities, effectively addresses the Dilemma of Differentiation. Difference (represented by the separate crayons with their distinct colors) and connectedness (represented by the colors' generative interrelatedness) each play a role (and of ultimately equal significance).

in ways that better reflect our uniquely human living complexities—and, when we do, to make the multiple kinds of new discernments that then become possible. Each of these conceptual steps is necessary if our thinking is to be sufficiently sophisticated to address the newly demanding challenges we now face in all parts of our personal and collective lives.

The Dilemma of Representation

Before we turn to more specific conceptual reflections, we should touch briefly on another basic quandary that inescapably presents itself when we step over Cultural Maturity's threshold. This additional quandary highlights an important reason why culturally mature understanding can be tricky to grasp. It also helps us further distinguish such understanding from results we might confuse it with. Creative Systems Theory calls it the *Dilemma of Representation*. It turns out that conventional approaches to both language and pictorial representation can easily get in the way when we try to depict where culturally mature systemic perspective takes us.

The fact that we encounter the Dilemma of Representation has nothing to do with the results of Cultural Maturity's changes being mysterious. Quite the opposite—it is a product of the necessary precision. But this outcome does mean that we need to take care when writing and thinking about Cultural Maturity's changes. The Dilemma of Representation intrudes whenever we wish to depict culturally mature concepts or results. It describes a limit we cannot escape.

In Chapter Two, I made reference to how the Dilemma of Representation confronts us when it comes to pictorial representation when I observed that representational sleight of hand is required when using the doorway image to depict "bridging." (I noted that while "bridging" might seem to be best represented by the doorway's lintel, the kind of "bridging" we have interest in involves stepping between the columns and into the new territory beyond.) The box-of-crayons image employs a similar sleight of hand. The crayons' differing hues along with the implied presence of the artist's involvement are what make this representation work. Creative Systems Theory calls images that succeed in this way "three-plus" representation. They use two dimensions (that imply three) to depict phenomena that three dimensions alone cannot capture. Good "three-plus" images are rare. I am always delighted when I find one that works.

The more verbal aspect of the Dilemma of Representation has influenced the writing of this book in multiple ways, often behind the scenes. For example, I have often phrased statements in unusual ways. Conventions of grammar are products of their times in culture and this is certainly true with modern usage. A prime example concerns sentence structure. We have two basic kinds available to us, each of which implies a certain (and now-familiar) kind of causal relationship. We have "active" constructions, which tend to imply mechanistic causality (verbs affect nouns in a cause-and-effect manner). And we have "passive" constructions that emphasize simple connectedness (a rose is a rose).[19] I've at least tried to be sure that my style of writing doesn't suggest relationships and causalities that run counter to what I am trying to communicate.

Another thing I've done to get beyond the Dilemma of Representation is to draw on figures of speech—for example, in using phrases like "the whole ball of wax" and "getting our minds around a question's complexity" to suggest systemic understanding. A key reason that familiar approaches to representation leave us short is that a full understanding of any culturally mature concept requires that we draw on multiple intelligences. Because figures of speech bring multiple intelligences into language, they can help us get beyond the Dilemma of Representation's limitations (although we must choose figures of speech well and apply them precisely).

The Dilemma of Representation has also come into play with my emphasis on apparent contradictions. I've noted, for example, how culturally mature truth is both more complex and simpler than what it replaces, how culturally mature perspective makes us uncompromisingly respectful of real limitation and also able to see beyond such constraints, and how the kind of systemic understanding we have interest in increases our appreciation for both difference and connectedness. While the opposite poles of each of these contradictions are readily described, the Dilemma of Representation immediately confronts us when we attempt to depict

---

19 A strict grammarian might object that "a rose is a rose" is not a formally passive construction. Perhaps we might better speak of more rational and more poetic construction, or construction that emphasizes difference versus that which emphasizes connectedness.

how culturally mature systemic perspective provides a larger picture. Often the best I've been able to do is point in the general direction in which more integrative interpretations are to be found.

The Dilemma of Representation intrudes not just when we try to depict human systems. Philosopher and semanticist Alfred Korzybski pointed toward this conundrum early in the last century and tied it to difficulties we encounter whenever we attempt to describe life. In his words: "Any organism must be treated as-a-whole.... It is seemingly little realized, at present, that this simple and innocent-looking statement involves a fully structural revisioning of our language."[20] We recognize the Dilemma of Representation with purely physical systems in the impossibility of conventionally representing concepts like those of quantum mechanics. Does the Dilemma of Representation then reflect something inherent to existence? What we can know for sure is that this difficulty inherently accompanies how we are coming to understand (though we would hope that changes in how we understand are taking us at least a bit closer to thinking in ways that reflect how things actually work).

Along with helping us further appreciate the conceptual stretch that culturally mature understanding requires, the Dilemma of Representation also provides an important tool for evaluating the success of efforts toward such understanding. Mechanistic formulations may be complicated, but they can be explicitly represented (at least mathematically) if our depictions have sufficient detail. Systemic formulations that emphasize connectedness and ultimate oneness can't be represented, but for a very different reason than that which we encounter with culturally mature systemic conception. In making mystery primary, they make ultimate truth, by definition, invisible. Recognizing the Dilemma of Representation's specific kind of quandary helps alert us to when a particular formulation may provide the kind of assistance we are looking for.

In the end, there is nothing obscure—or even really complicated— about the fact that we encounter the Dilemma of Representation. It is a simple consequence of the more sophisticated kind of understanding

---

20 Korzybski, Alfred, *Collected Works 1920-1950*, Institute for General Semantics, 1990

we have interest in. It comes part and parcel with engaging experience with the whole of who we are—in particular with our multiple intelligences. Culturally mature perspective draws on the complex richness of our inner makeup, and in the process helps us better appreciate the complex richness of existence more generally. When we view reality through a culturally mature lens, like it or not, the Dilemma of Representation comes with the territory.[21]

"Creative Systems" Understanding

Let's now look briefly at one particular truth framework that successfully meets Cultural Maturity's demands. I've described how Creative Systems Theory underlies this book's ideas about cultural change. Creative Systems Theory gives the argument for Cultural Maturity an important further level of precision. It also provides important additional insight into the general kind of thinking that Cultural Maturity's cognitive changes make possible. (Creative System Theory's systemic approach successfully addresses the Dilemma of Differentiation and offers a way of thinking that helps us get our minds beyond the Dilemma of Representation.)

This briefest of introductory looks at Creative Systems Theory's approach will require going beyond the general scope of this short book and covering some conceptually complicated material in a highly abbreviated fashion. Here is where we necessarily really go lickety-split. You can feel free to skim this section and the next if theory is not where your primary interest lies. Creative Systems Theory's particular formulations are not needed to make effective use of the concept of Cultural Maturity. But people who wish to have the argument for the concept's conclusions made as rigorous as possible, or who are intrigued by the question of what detailed culturally mature conception might look like, may find these more specific theoretical reflections of particular interest.[22]

These reflections will focus on two implications of Creative Systems Theory that have particular pertinence for this inquiry. In this

---

21 See *Cultural Maturity: A Guidebook for the Future* for a more detailed look at the Dilemma of Representation.

22 The Institute for Creative Development website (www.CreativeSystems. org) contains multiple links to Creative Systems Theory–related material.

section, we will look at how the theory provides an important illustration of how culturally mature perspective can be translated into broadly applicable and highly nuanced formulations—detailed, whole-box-of-crayons conceptual tools. The book's next section uses Creative Systems Theory to provide insight into how change in human systems works. Of particular importance, these additional reflections will make the Dilemma of Trajectory more explicit, and also further clarify how Cultural Maturity's changes provide a way beyond it.

We need to start with some basic background. Creative Systems Theory has its foundation in an attempt to answer a key question implied in this chapter's reflections: What is it that makes us humans highly unusual, if not unique, as living systems? Creative Systems Theory proposes that what ultimately separates us from the rest of the planet's creatures is the audacity of our creative capacities—the depth and all-encompassing persistence of our toolmaking natures. We are prodigious makers of things, certainly. We are also makers of ideas and social systems, and perhaps most important, makers of meaning.

Creative Systems Theory uses this observation to develop an encompassing conceptual framework that helps us make sense of purpose, change, and interrelationship in human systems. The theory describes how human understanding, and in the end, human experience as a whole, organizes creatively. (It uses the word "creative" in a specific—or we might say particularly general—sense, to refer not just to invention or artistic expression, but to formative process as it manifests in every part of our lives.) The theory goes on to propose that part of what makes our time in culture's evolving story unique is that we are becoming newly capable of appreciating how this might be so. Creative Systems Theory describes how Cultural Maturity's cognitive changes allow us to more consciously engage the whole of ourselves as toolmaking beings. In doing so, we become more aware of our creative natures and more cognizant of how our inherently generative, toolmaking cognitive mechanisms work.

The idea that formative process is somehow central to human experience is not original to Creative Systems Theory. At the beginning of this chapter I quoted Alfred North Whitehead's claim that "creativity is the universal of universals." This assertion lay at the heart of his

Process Philosophy.[23] Philosopher of science Karl Popper proposed that "the greatest riddle of cosmology may well be … that the universe is, in a sense, creative."[24] We can also find references to creative organization—at least references of a metaphorical sort—by looking back through history. We have always given our explanations of how things come to be—ancient creation myths, modern monotheism's various stories of genesis, science's Big Bang—special status.

Creative Systems Theory affirms the basic recognition that creative process has pivotal significance, then takes the critical further step of making a creative frame the basis for a comprehensive and practical set of conceptual tools. These tools have implications for understanding as a whole—for making sense of our physical and biological worlds as well as ourselves—but their primary focus is on human systems.[25] The theory describes how formative process's mechanisms underlie human experience of every sort, the patterns that result, and how those patterns make us who we are.

A few "snapshot" observations that look at Creative Systems Theory in application make these results more concrete. Creative Systems Theory concepts directly address each of the new kinds of truth distinctions that I've proposed are becoming newly important—and newly possible—with Cultural Maturity's changes. They include ideas that address truth at its most basic—that help us think and act from the whole of what makes something true (whole-box-of-crayons truths)—as well as concepts that help us discern and articulate more detailed and contextually specific kinds of truth (crayon-specific truths). Creative Systems

---

23 To further quote Whitehead: "The ultimate metaphysical ground is the creative advance into novelty … both God and the world are in [its] grip." (See Whitehead, Alfred North, *Process and Reality*, New York, Free Press, 1978.)

24 Popper, Karl, *The Open Universe*, Routledge, London and New York, 1991

25 At least Creative Systems Theory helps us make sense of why we have understood the inanimate and nature in the very different ways we have through history. But it also invites more encompassing reflection about how to best understand these various aspects of experience today. (In *Quick and Dirty Answers to the Biggest of Questions*, I suggest that we might best think of it all as like Neapolitan ice cream—each layer of existence fundamentally different, yet at once an aspect of a larger, specifically "creative" picture.)

Theory describes how we can address each of these kinds of new systemic concepts (including both change-related and here-and-now kinds of crayon-specific truths) by framing them creatively. Because a creative frame has its roots in what ultimately makes us who we are, it reconciles the Dilemma of Differentiation. For this same reason, the concepts that result, while complex in their implications, can be strikingly concise. They also produce a kind of precision hard to achieve in other ways.

Creative Systems Theory calls systemic notions that address truth at its most fundamental *Whole-System Patterning Concepts*. The most basic such notion—for our purposes, we can call it simply "aliveness"—addresses truth in the sense I referred to in Chapter Five when I observed that culturally mature moral choice measures the degree to which an act is life-affirming.[26] Put that observation in motion, and moral choice becomes a reflection of acts that support the most ultimately creative engagement with experience (using the word "creative" in that most encompassing sense). Think of truth as the point of an arrow or a compass point we use to guide us forward. Creative Systems Theory proposes that this most basic of whole-box systemic notions is where we necessarily start when culturally defined guideposts stop providing useful measures of truth and value.

Another Whole-System Patterning Concept, what Creative Systems Theory calls *Capacitance*, measures a system's overall health and well-being—its capacity to engage life. Think of a balloon and how much air it can hold before bursting.[27] The concept of Capacitance draws a circle around more particular measures of capacity such as intelligence, inventiveness, spiritual development, and emotional sophistication.[28]

---

26 Creative Systems Theory calls this most basic truth concern the *Question of Referent*. It calls measures like "aliveness" *Integrative Referents*.

27 Or with human systems, before it responds protectively. In Chapter Two, I observed that systems tend to polarize when they face challenges beyond what they can handle. More formally we could say they tend to reactively polarize when they face challenges that require more then their available Capacitance.

28 The concept of Capacitance has an important relationship to more change-related notions in that Capacitance is the one thing that increases consistently over the course of any developmental process. I like to think

Creative Systems Theory calls the first kind of more detailed, con-text-specific truth—the change-related sort—*Patterning in Time*. Cre-ative Patterning in Time concepts give us the particular developmental notions I draw on in this volume. I've described how thinking about cultural change as evolutionary, at least in any useful sense, is new. Modern Age assumptions limit us to simple cause-and-effect think-ing. Developmental notions, certainly of the sort needed to describe human change with the needed dynamism and subtlety, necessarily draw on a more life-filled—and human life–filled—picture of change's mechanisms. Creative Systems Patterning in Time ideas describe how human formative processes of all sorts—what happens in an act of invention or artistic creation, the growth of a human relationship, individual human development, or the evolution of social systems— follow a related kind of generative progression. In other writings, I describe how this is so in detail. [29]

Creative Systems calls more here-and-now context-specific truth concepts *Patterning in Space*. Patterning in Space notions help us dis-

---

of the periodic times of reorganization that happen in human development as similar to what we see with how a snake, in order to grow, must now and then shed its skin. The skins that need to be shed represent stage-specific belief systems; the snake's expanding girth represents Capacitance. The concept of Capacitance has direct pertinence to understanding Cultural Maturity's changes and what they ask of us. I've described how, when we are ready for them, Cultural Maturity's new capacities are often not as difficult to acquire as we might think. At a certain Capacitance they become rather self-evident—part of our times' "new common sense."

Capacitance is also pertinent to Cultural Maturity in the necessary role it plays in evaluating whether a thought or action is mature in the needed new sense. Our reference in such evaluation can't be whether a thought or action fits within a particular set of beliefs. (Beliefs, in and of themselves, don't define Cultural Maturity.) Neither can we use as our reference whether the thought or action is broadly recognized or acclaimed. (Otherwise reality TV or the latest pop sensation should get our vote.) In the end, we have to use as our basis for evaluation the Capacitance that a particular thought or action reflects.

29 See *The Creative Imperative*, *Cultural Maturity: A Guidebook for the Future*, *Quick and Dirty Answers to the Biggest of Questions*, or the Creative Systems Theory website, www.CSTHome.org.

tinguish one systemic "crayon" from another and effectively manage and apply our "I contain multitudes" human multiplicities as they exist at a particular point in time. We can use Creative Systems Theory Patterning in Space notions to better understand conflicting ideologies (of the opposing here-and-now sort), to tease apart multiple aspects of our psychological functioning (such as the differing roles our various intelligences play), to make sense of how remarkably different individual human beings can be from one another (the Creative Systems Personality Typology provides a particularly nuanced framework for understanding personality style differences[30]), or to appreciate how various domains of culture—education, science, art, religion, or government—relate to one another.

---

30 See *Cultural Maturity: A Guidebook for the Future*, *The Power of Diversity*, or the Creative Systems Personality Typology website (www.CSPTHome.org). Earlier I observed that I find relationships between people of different temperaments increasingly common and promised a possible explanation. The Creative Systems Personality Typology describes how different temperaments preferentially embody specific parts of creative complexity (the sensibilities that different temperaments most draw on reflect different crayons in the systemic box). One result is that when Cultural Maturity's more Whole-System kind of understanding becomes timely, people of temperaments different from our own add to who we are in a whole new sense. At the very least, they always have things to teach us.

I find it remarkable that we have not before been cognizant of how profoundly different the experience of people with different personality styles can be. But if deep appreciation for authentic difference requires culturally mature perspective, blindness of this sort is what we would expect to find historically. Today, such blindness has major consequences, and not just when it comes to making relationships work. For example, that we don't more consciously take into account personality styles differences in education badly shortchanges many students. Similarly, psychology and psychotherapy suffer significantly from the fact that personality style differences are not more deeply appreciated. We often find differences that have primarily to do with temperament interpreted as psychopathology. And that we don't routinely factor in temperament differences when doing psychological research makes a great deal of such research largely useless. (That we don't factor in such differences when doing medical research certainly raises interesting questions. We have only recently begun to appreciate how we can't simply lump men and women together when studying disease processes. Because temperament differences are almost never taken into account, we may similarly be missing important information.)

Creative Systems, Polarity, and Intelligence

For this inquiry, the way Creative Systems Theory helps us understand change in human systems has particular importance. Here we take a brief closer look at two now familiar themes—polarity's role in understanding and the multifaceted nature of intelligence—that relate directly to a creative framing of change in human systems. These observations will add conceptual rigor to the developmental parallels that I've drawn on in making the argument for Cultural Maturity by clarifying how they reflect parallels we see with human formative processes of all sorts. They also provide important further evidence for my claim that something like what the concept of Cultural Maturity describes will be necessary if we are to effectively go forward. Each topic in a different way solidifies the argument for the Dilemma of Trajectory. Each also confirms how Cultural Maturity's changes both resolve the dilemma and offer important new possibility.

Polarity and Creative Change

The basic fact that we encounter polarity provides one of the best ways to recognize the creative ingredient in how human systems work.[31] A simple recognition gets us started: We find that creative poles, rather than just being opposite to one another, reflect a particular kind of symmetry. We can speak of that symmetry in a variety of ways. Most simply, we could say that polar relationships have complementary right and left hands. With polarity's "right hand" we find harder, often more rational and more material qualities. With polarity's "left hand" we find qualities of a softer, more poetic sort. Facts juxtapose with feelings, mind with body, material with spiritual, and so on. We see this symmetry suggested in how I represented the doorway image in Figure 2-1. The column on

---

31 We commonly use the term "polarity" to refer to several different but related types of conceptual juxtapositions. Some polarities are most defined by opposition—for example, the us-versus-them polarities of warfare. With other polarities, the relationship is more of a "separate worlds" sort—for example, with the polarity of objective versus subjective. We often then speak of duality rather than polarity. We also use the word "polarity" to include juxtaposition, such as that between rhythm and melody in music, in which "opposite" elements are expressly complementary. Creative Systems Theory describes how these differences in the character of polarity reflect time- and space-specific creative dynamics.

the left is labeled with more "left-hand" characteristics (art, the sacred, nature …), the column on the right with more "right-hand" characteristics (science, the secular, humanity …).

Psychology has terms for these extremes that are drawn from the study of myth. It refers to the more concrete side of each pairing as "archetypally masculine" and its softer counterpart as "archetypally feminine." The gender-linked language can cause confusion, particularly today as women and men each seek to make both poles their own, but its sexual connotations are evocative. In some fundamental way, the relationship between polar extremes becomes "procreative."

The answer to an obvious, but rarely asked question, makes the relationship between creativity and polarity even more explicit. It also helps put polarity's picture in generative motion. That question: Why do we think in the language of polarity in the first place (in other words, why do we think of experience as anything but whole)? Creative Systems Theory proposes that the generation of polarity is necessary to anything creative.

Think of what happens in the creative process that produces a new idea. Any such process begins in an "original unity" of established knowledge. Next, an insight breaks off from that unity and in doing so creates polarity. Over time, that newly created idea develops and matures. (See Figure 6-2.) The generation and evolution of polarity is intrinsic to how formative processes of every sort in human systems function. We wouldn't be who we are without it.

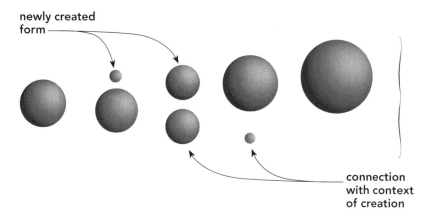

newly created form

connection with context of creation

Fig. 6-2. The Creative Generation of Polarity

To address the specific kind of change that produces second-half-of-life maturity in our individual lives—and by implication Cultural Maturity's changes—we need a further recognition. Any formative process has two halves. The first half brings the newly created object or idea into being and generates polarity. The second half reintegrates the now-developed and refined new object or idea with the context from which it originated. In doing so, it establishes a new, now-expanded whole. What had been a new insight in the process becomes "second nature" (and part of the context for further creative possibility). The "bridging" of polarities is one result. We can depict this as a simple three-step process, as shown in Figure 6-3.

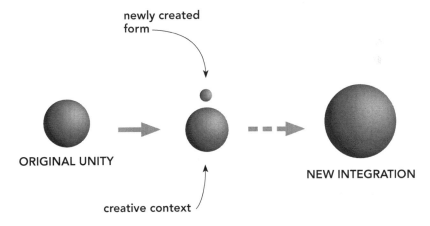

Fig. 6-3. Polarity and "Bridging" in Formative Process

To map human formative process, Creative Systems Theory puts these two pictures together and expands the result like the bellows of an accordian. (See the diagram in Figure 6-4.) The first half of formative process becomes an evolving play of polarities, with polarity in each stage following a predictable progression. Each succeeding stage reflects greater identification with the newly created form and diminishing identification with the context it came from. In the second half of formative process, the newly created form gradually finds mature integration with what has come before, with the outcome being a new, now expanded and more complete picture—a new common sense. Creative Systems Theory calls this generic template the *Creative Function*.

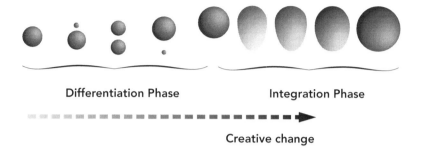

Differentiation Phase   **Integration Phase**

Creative change

Fig. 6-4. The Creative Function[32]

In other writings, I examine each creative stage in detail—what characterizes it as experience, how it alters the ways we relate to ourselves and others, how it brings with it particular ways of thinking and seeing the world. I also examine the ways in which this creative progression manifests with different kinds of human formative process—such as an act of invention, individual human development, the growth of a personal relationship, the development of a community or an organization, or the evolution of culture.[33]

For our purposes in this book, the basic idea that a creative frame helps us understand the workings of change in human systems is sufficient. But one additional polarity-related observation is worth noting both for its philosophical implications and because it serves as the basis for further important Creative Systems Theory concepts. It follows from this creative picture of polarity that a single polarity in

---

32 The whole of Creative Systems Theory can be understood in relation to the Creative Function. This depiction of the Creative Function is another example of "three-plus" representation.

33 See *Cultural Maturity: A Guidebook for the Future* or *Quick and Dirty Answers to the Biggest of Questions*. The developmental picture a creative frame describes is not as clean and predictable as this simple description might suggest. Change processes often happen in a two-steps-forward/one-step-back fashion. And formative processes can simply collapse at any point. But the general architecture the Creative Function describes holds up with remarkable consistency.

the end underlies all others: connectedness/unity on one hand juxta-posed with difference/multiplicity on the other.[34]

Because this recognition contains a particularly baffling apparent contradiction—it makes unity (which would seem to be about every-thing) half of a polarity—it can be hard for some people to get their minds around. But this chapter's observations about how polarities have an underlying symmetry helps us make sense of it. Another way of saying the same thing is that polarity at its most basic juxtaposes the extremes of left-hand and right-hand sensibility.

Philosophically, this recognition helps reconcile some of the most fundamental of conflicting beliefs—for example, those that can leave religion and science intractably at odds. Views that reduce truth to spiritual oneness and views that make the interacting-sepa-rate-parts notions of mechanistic science final truth (views that not only value science but that reflect a narrow scientism) come to rep-resent not so much differing beliefs as systemically counterpoised ideologies. They become opposite-hued "crayons" within the larger systemic box.[35]

Understanding polarity at its most basic also helps clarify a par-ticularly important apparent contradiction that I emphasized earlier: how culturally mature understanding increases our appreciation for both connectedness and difference. This result applies across the board—from how Cultural Maturity alters how we relate as indi-viduals and groups, to what happens when we "bridge" more abstract polarities such as mind and body, masculine and feminine, or even matter and energy. If polarity at its most fundamental juxtaposes connectedness/unity on one hand with difference/multiplicity on the other, and "bridging," rather than producing compromise, results in a deepened appreciation for each polar aspect's unique contribu-tion to possibility, then this result is exactly what we would expect to find. From culturally mature understanding's more systemic vantage,

---

34 *Cultural Maturity: A Guidebook for the Future* examines this observation in greater detail.

35 See *Quick and Dirty Answers to the Biggest of Questions* for more specific thoughts about how Cultural Maturity's changes might alter how we think about both religion and science.

connectedness and difference become aspects of a larger picture. They also each derive new emphasis, and come to be seen in ways that are newly consequential.

This creative framing of polarity at its most basic provides the basis for one of Creative Systems Theory's most useful tools for identifying traps in our thinking. Creative Systems Theory calls beliefs that identify with connectedness *Unity Fallacies*, beliefs that identify with difference *Separation Fallacies*, and beliefs that split the difference *Compromise Fallacies*. Creative Systems Theory delineates how we find characteristic types of each kind of fallacy with different personality styles and with each stage in formative process.[36]

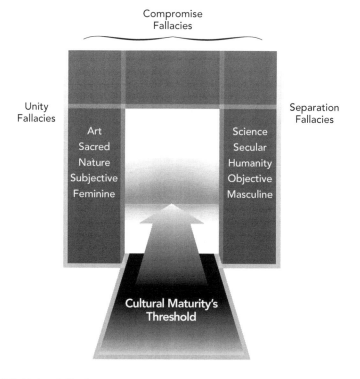

Fig. 6-5. Polar Fallacies

_____

36 See *Cultural Maturity: A Guidebook for the Future* for a more detailed examination of tools that can help us identity traps in our thinking.

Multiple Intelligences and Creative Change

The multifaceted nature of intelligence adds important flesh to this bare-bones picture of formative process. I've described how culturally mature understanding and actions require that we apply more aspects of intelligence—more of our diverse ways of knowing—than we've traditionally used at one time. Creative Systems Theory describes how our various intelligences are, in the end, creatively related. It is a notion that should not take us by surprise if our toolmaking nature is what most defines us.

Creative Systems Theory proposes that we are uniquely creative creatures not just because we have conscious awareness, but also because of the particular ways in which various aspects of our intelligence work and how they interrelate.[37] It describes how our various intelligences—or we might say "sensibilities," to better reflect all they encompass—together function to support and drive creative change.[38] It delineates how different ways of knowing—and different relationships between ways of knowing—predominate at specific times in any human change process. Creative Systems Theory also ties the underlying structures of intelligence to patterns we see in how human systems change—thereby both helping us better understand change and hinting at the possibility that we might better predict change.

I've described how Creative Systems Theory identifies four basic types of intelligence: body intelligence, imagination, emotional intelligence, and the rational. Creative Systems Theory proposes that these various modes of intelligence, juxtaposed like colors on a color wheel, function together as creativity's mechanism. That wheel, like the wheel of a car or a Ferris wheel, is continually turning, continually

---

37 Creative Systems Theory's picture of multiple intelligences is unusual both for its emphasis on change and for the attention it gives to how various cognitive aspects work together.

38 Which is not to say that our diverse intelligences don't at times work at cross-purposes to one another. Often they arrive at conflicting conclusions—sometimes because they simply do, but also often because conflict is a natural and necessary part of an underlying developmental dynamic. (For example, internal wars between thoughts and emotions are essential to the developmental tasks of adolescence.)

in motion. The way in which the facets of intelligence juxtapose makes change—and specifically purposeful change—inherent in our natures. The diagram in Figure 6-6 shows these links between the workings of intelligence and the stages of formative process.

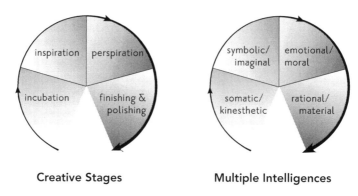

Creative Stages   Multiple Intelligences

Fig. 6-6. Formative Process and Intelligence

A brief look at a single creative process—let's take as an example the writing of a book such as this one—helps clarify how this works. In subtly overlapping and multilayered ways, the process by which this book came to be took me through a progression of creative stages and associated sensibilities. Creative processes unfold in varied ways, but the following outline is generally representative.

> Before beginning to write, my sense of the book is murky at best. (Creative processes begin in darkness.) I am aware that I have ideas I want to communicate. But I have only the most beginning sense of just what ideas I want to include, or how I want to address them. This is creativity's "incubation" stage. The dominant in- telligence here is the kinesthetic—body intelligence, if you will. When I am in this phase, it is like I am pregnant, but don't yet know with what. What I do know takes the form of "inklings" and faint "glimmerings," inner sensings. If I want to feed this part of the creative process, I do things that help me to be reflective and to connect in my body. I take a long walk in the woods, draw a warm bath, build a fire in the fireplace.

Generativity's second stage propels the new thing created out of darkness into first light. With the book, I begin to have "ah-has"—my mind floods with notions about what I might express in the book and possible approaches for expression. Some of these "inspiration stage" insights take the form of thoughts. Others manifest more as images or metaphors. Here the dominant intelligence is the imaginal—that which most defines art, myth, and the let's-pretend world of young children. The products of this period in the creative process may appear suddenly—as with Archimedes's "eureka"—or they may come more subtly and gradually. It is this stage, and this part of our larger sensibility, that we tend to most traditionally associate with things creative.[39]

The third stage leaves behind the realm of first possibilities and takes us into the world of tangible, manifest form. With the book, I try out specific structural approaches. And I get down to the hard work of writing and revising—and writing and revising some more. This is creation's "perspiration" stage. The dominant intelligence is different still, more emotional and visceral—the intelligence of heart and guts. It is here that we confront the hard work of finding the right approach and the most satisfying means of expression. We also confront limits to our skills and are challenged to push beyond them. The perspiration stage tends to bring a new moral commitment and emotional edginess. We must compassionately but unswervingly confront what we have created if it is to stand the test of time.

Generativity's fourth stage is more concerned with detail and refinement. While the book's basic form is established, much yet remains to do. Both the book's ideas and how they are expressed need a more fine-toothed examination. Rational intelligence

---

39 Because the imaginal indirectly anticipates final form, there is a sense in which it foreshadows fact. I am reminded of Rilke's poetic reflection that "The future enters into us in order to transform us long before it happens"—an observation about both creative process and understanding's broader generativity.

orders this "finishing and polishing" stage. This period is more conscious and more concerned with aesthetic precision than the previous periods. It is also more concerned with audience and outcome. It brings final focus to the creative work, and offers the clarity of thought and nuances of style needed for effective communication.

Creative expression is often placed in the world at this point. But a further stage—or more accurately, an additional series of stages—remains. This next phase is as important as any of the others—and of particular significance with mature creative process. It varies greatly in length and intensity. This further generative sequence is what Creative Systems Theory refers to as *Creative Integration*. With the process of refinement complete, we can now step back from the work and appreciate it with new perspective. We become better able to recognize the relationship of one part to another. And we can better appreciate the relationship of the work to its creative contexts, to ourselves, and to the time and place in which it was created. We might call creativity's integrative stages the "seasoning" or "ripening" stages.

Creative Integration forms a complement to the more differentiation-defined tasks of earlier stages—a second half to the creative process. Creative Integration is about learning to use our diverse ways of knowing more consciously together. It is about applying our intelligences in various combinations and balances as called for by the time and situation. It is also about a growing ability not just to engage the work as a whole, but to draw on *ourselves* as a whole in relationship to it. Because wholeness is where we started—before the disruptive birth of new creation—in a sense, Creative Integration returns us to where we began. But because change that matters changes everything, this is a point of beginning that is new—it has not existed before.

Creative Systems Theory applies this relationship between intelligence and formative process to human understanding as a whole. It proposes that the same general progression of sensibilities we see with a creative project also orders the creative growth of all human systems. It argues that we see similar patterns at all levels—from the growth of an individual, to how relationships evolve, to the development of an organization, to culture and its evolution. To illustrate, here are a few brief associations that focus on individual and cultural development, the formative processes that have been our primary concerns:

- The same bodily intelligence that orders creative "incubation" plays a particularly prominent role in the infant's rhythmic world of movement, touch, and taste. The realities of early tribal cultures also draw deeply on body sensibilities. Truth in tribal societies is synonymous with the rhythms of nature and—through dance, song, story, and drumbeat—with the body of the tribe.

- The same imaginal intelligence that we saw ordering creative "inspiration" takes prominence in the play-centered world of the young child. We also hear its voice with particular strength in early civilizations—such as in ancient Greece or Egypt, with the Incas and Aztecs in the Americas, or in the classical East— with their mythic pantheons and great symbolic tales.

- The same emotional and moral intelligence that orders creative "perspiration" tends to occupy center stage in adolescence with its deepening passions and pivotal struggles for identity. It can be felt with particular strength also in the beliefs and values of the European Middle Ages, times marked by feudal struggle and ardent moral conviction (and today, in places where struggle and conflict seem to be forever recurring).

- The same rational intelligence that comes forward for the "finishing and polishing" tasks of creativity takes new prominence in young adulthood, as we strive to create our unique place in the world of adult expectations. This more refined and refining aspect of intelligence stepped to the fore culturally in the West with the Renaissance and the Age of Reason, and has held sway into modern times.

■ Finally, and especially relevant to the concept of Cultural Maturity, the same more consciously integrative intelligence that we see in the "seasoning" stage of a creative act orders the unique developmental capacities—the wisdom—of a lifetime's second half. Culturally, we can see this same more integrative relationship with intelligence just beneath the surface in advances that have transformed understanding in the West through the last century.

We associate the Age of Reason with Descartes's assertion that "I think, therefore I am." We could make a parallel assertion for each of the other cultural stages referred to in these observations: "I am embodied, therefore I am"; "I imagine, therefore I am"; "I am a moral being, therefore I am"; and, if the concept of Cultural Maturity is accurate, "I understand maturely and systemically—with the whole of myself—therefore I am." Cultural Maturity proposes that these observations about intelligence's creative workings were possible because such consciously integrative dynamics are reordering how we think and perceive.[40]

Creative Change and the Dilemma of Trajectory

For our purposes, these reflections on the creative role of polarity and on intelligence's formative mechanisms at least provide further insight into the kind of systemic thinking that I have drawn on in arriving at the conclusions in this book. They also provide important, more specifically theoretical layers to the argument for Cultural Maturity and its changes. With both polarity and intelligence, we witness the specifically integrative kind of process needed for culturally mature perspective.

As significant is the way each of these descriptions supports my claim that the kind of change that the concept of Cultural Maturity describes

---

40 Note a surprising theoretical implication of this evolving picture: I've described the fact of multiple intelligences as a Patterning in Space, here-and-now sort of crayon-specific recognition. But just as much, it concerns change and the patterns that underlie how change in human systems take place. Creative Systems Theory is unique in linking change concepts and here-and-now difference concepts in this way.

represents not just one possible option going forward, but the only kind of option that can work. In Chapter Five, I described how the evolution of polarity and the evolution of intelligence each confront us with the Dilemma of Trajectory. This section's more detailed picture of how formative processes evolve makes these confrontations explicit.

I've proposed that continuing forward as we have threatens to sever us from essential aspects of what makes us human. Using the language of polarity, this includes any of the softer, more "left-hand," more archetypally feminine aspects of human experience—the artistic, the spiritual, the world of children, or the receptive[41] more generally. Described in terms of ways of knowing, this includes anything that draws on the more creatively germinal dimensions of intelligence—the body, the imagination, or the more fragile, beginning aspects of emotional sensibility.[42] We can understand the various Transitional Absurdities that I listed in the previous chapter as reflections of what happens when we lose any depth of connection with these essential facets of our human natures. The unending superficiality of mass material culture reflects a reality in which buying things has become a glamorized last refuge for the receptive. And our amazing capacity to ignore damage to the environment and our alienation from our bodies reflect our modern disconnect from intelligence's more primordial sensibilities in particularly graphic ways.

---

41 Notice that we really don't even have language for the receptive in modern times. The opposite of active becomes merely passive.

42 For this distancing to fully make sense, we need the added recognition that moving from one stage to the next involves not just a necessary leap in understanding, but also the creation of amnesias for realities we have moved beyond. Thus adolescents tend to find the realities of children quite baffling, even though by all rights, having just left these more imagination-based realities behind, they should be the world's great experts on them. Similarly, young adults tend to find adolescent thoughts and actions not just immature, but nonsensical. In the first half of formative processes, we actively distance ourselves from the more creatively germinal/primordial aspects of our being. These developmentally necessary amnesias gradually dissolve with formative process's mature stages. (See *Cultural Maturity: A Guidebook for the Future* for a closer look at why we see developmental amnesias and how they play out in related ways over the course of any human formative process.)

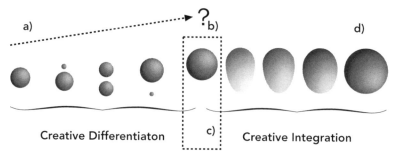

a) Cultural evolution's trajectory to this point

b) Transition (with right-hand sensibility at its peak and left-hand sensibilities largely eclipsed)

c) The Dilemma of Trajectory (with Cultural Maturity, or some similarly integrative process, needed to go on)

d) How Cultural Maturity reconciles the Dilemma of Trajectory

Fig. 6-7. The Dilemma of Trajectory

These dynamics put the Dilemma of Trajectory and what could appear to be dead-end circumstances into high relief. In doing so, they also support the conclusion that Cultural Maturity—or at least something that can produce a similar kind of integrative result—provides the only viable way forward. With regard to polarity, we've seen how culturally mature perspective brings an equal valuing of left-hand and right-hand qualities. It also makes overt the fact that each half of fundamental polarity is necessary to the other's significance. And nothing more defines Cultural Maturity's cognitive reordering than the ability to draw more consciously and explicitly on intelligence's multiple, "creative" aspects.

It is hard to conceive of a future we would want to live in without at least the beginnings of such more integrative, whole-box-of-crayons understanding. With it, we not only gain the capacity to make better choices, we better recognize the ultimate creativity of our natures and affirm the possibility of new creative options in times ahead.

Understanding Cultural Change

We don't need Creative Systems Theory's specific formulations to arrive at the concept of Cultural Maturity—the developmental analogy will suffice. But a solid sense of the general "developmental/ evolutionary' kind of thinking the concept draws on helps us distinguish the concept of Cultural Maturity from notions that might seem similar. I will conclude this chapter's theoretical observations with a few such compare-and-contrast reflections. I will first touch briefly on how the general kind of thinking I have applied is different in the basic way it views cultural change and the course of history. I will then turn to differences that have more specifically to do with the tasks ahead.[43]

We should start with objections to the whole evolutionary perspective endeavor. Early on, I observed how ideas that describe culture in evolutionary terms meet immediate resistance in some circles, and I promised to expand on this observation. Academic thinkers often dismiss such ideas out of hand. At least in part, this reflects hard-learned lessons. Evolutionary ideas have been used to justify some of history's most despicable beliefs and actions. Georg Hegel's philosophically idealist formulations—which cast a mythically elevated Prussian state as culture's culminating expression (and purportedly later influenced the thinking of Adolf Hitler)—are most often cited.[44] Evolutionary notions also confront postmodern thought's common, and at least partly justified, general wariness toward big-picture ideas. Overarching historical ideas have too often lumped together topics that have no business being placed in the same pot.

But it should now be clear that we need to better understand how cultural systems change—if for no other reason than that we need to do so if we are to get along in a globally interconnected world. I've proposed that cultures grow and evolve in predictable ways—not in a lockstep

---

43 See *Cultural Maturity: A Guidebook for the Future* and the various Creative Systems–related websites for more detailed "compare and contrast" examinations.

44 Analysis rooted in philosophical idealism views history as progressing toward some final ideal—sometimes political, other times more spiritual. One result is that such thinking can be readily used to justify the elevation of one's own kind and the denigration of others. (In an upcoming footnote, I briefly address how philosophical idealism works and why its formulations ultimately fail us.)

manner, but predictably nonetheless. While the specifics of any framework that suggests developmental stages are legitimately questioned, I
think the evidence for developmental pattern is, in fact, close to irrefut-
able. Beyond the depth at which parallels appear to work and the practical problem-solving power that this recognition of pattern provides,
there is also the difficulty of conceiving of a future we would want to live
in if such pattern does not hold. If the concept of Cultural Maturity is
accurate, cultural evolution should produce significant change in times
ahead—and change with real and important promise.

I find it useful to divide how the general kind of evolutionary perspective applied in this book contrasts with other ways of thinking
about change in cultural systems into a layered series of differences.
The first kind of difference should go without saying, but we need to
acknowledge it if the word "evolutionary" is not to get in our way:
What I describe is evolutionary change of a specifically cultural sort.
This difference is critical to thinking effectively about the future. For
example, I've heard people use an evolutionary argument to claim
that we as humans have always been warlike, and that this will never
change. In reaching this conclusion, they miss that evolution has two
meanings. There is biological evolution, and on that front we are unlikely to see much that will help us. But there is also cultural evolution: the ways in which social systems grow and evolve over time.
Cultural evolution—certainly as framed here—supports some very
different kinds of outcomes.

A next kind of difference distinguishes the kind of evolutionary
perspective we've drawn on from most views that acknowledge that
cultures do change over time. Conventionally, if people have thought
of culture as evolving at all, they've framed this evolution in terms
of invention-related advances—a time of hunter-gatherers, an age of
agriculture, a modern Industrial Age. Views that think of cultural evolution solely in terms of technological change can contribute to understanding, but they provide limited assistance at best when it comes
to the future. At the very least, we must recognize that inventing and
using inventions wisely are not at all the same. And views that define advancement wholly in technological terms provide no help at all
with addressing the Dilemma of Trajectory—indeed, they easily blind
us to its presence.

In these pages, we've focused our attention on changes in how we humans *understand and act*. In fact, thinking in terms of invention-related advances and thinking in terms of changes in how we understand and act are not as different as we might assume. In the end, what we create reflects what we are becoming capable of understanding. And new invention, in turn, helps drive the creative evolution of understanding.[45] But if our thinking is to effectively address the future, it must give as much attention to changes in us—we who are doing the inventing—as it does to the particular products of our toolmaking capacities.

Finally, we need to recognize essential differences that distinguish the developmental/evolutionary kind of perspective we have drawn on from other views that give primary attention to change at the level of how we think and engage our worlds. The ideas of historians who have attempted to tease out such patterns have largely gone out of favor through the previous century, and often for good reasons, as noted earlier. If they haven't served to falsely idealize, they've drawn on perceived associations that haven't held up to scrutiny. Such ideas have also gone out of favor for a reason that has nothing to do with the usefulness of the approach. They've tended to be set aside as part of the general push toward more hard science–like methods in the social sciences.

Culturally mature perspective lauds efforts to cleanse historical analysis of ideological influences, but it also makes clear that we really can't stop with this "objectivist" kind of methodology. I've described the essential role that an appreciation for multiple intelligences plays with mature systemic understanding. Without the more integrative kind of understanding that Cultural Maturity's cognitive changes provide, it is very hard to discern pattern in any deep sense.[46]

---

45 For example, the mechanistic worldview that accompanied Modern Age understanding provided the necessary conceptual context for the flowering of Europe's Industrial Revolution. And Industrial Age advances in turn gave us the supporting structures for our modern individualist way of life. Arguably, our time's emerging, more dynamic and systemic ways of understanding and the best of today's Digital Age advances interplay in a similarly co-causal manner.

46 Earlier I observed that evolutionary perspective can meet immediate resistance in the academic world. Besides the very real problems with past

Certain more recent formulations again apply a "changes in how
we understand and act" approach, and some do so in ways that better
acknowledge multiple ways of knowing. I think in particular of interpretations that emphasize needed "new paradigms" in understanding.
Often such formulations provide important insights and may usefully
complement this inquiry.[47] But it is important to appreciate that such
interpretations can also include particularly unhelpful ideas. For example, when it comes to notions that have to do specifically with how
cultural systems change, we often find beliefs that in the end represent
only new forms of philosophical idealism (most often, in this case, of
the more spiritual sort). In contrast, developmental/evolutionary perspective has nothing to do with idealized destinations. Cultural Maturity describes a natural, "common sense" next chapter in culture's
ongoing story. [48]

---

approaches that I noted, there is also a more basic, largely unconscious
explanation. We can't entertain evolutionary ideas—at least of the sort that
come with culturally mature perspective—without bringing into question
the assumption—common with the modern academic enterprise—that
rationality represents truth's ultimate arbiter.

47 See *Cultural Maturity: A Guidebook for the Future*.

48 Thinking that gets described in "new paradigm" terms also includes ideas
that reduce ultimately to new versions of liberal/humanist or philosophically
romantic interpretation. The fact that we might see confusion with these
particular kinds of ideas is understandable, even if it is decidedly unhelpful.
Each shares with the other that it gives special emphasis to more left-hand
aspects of truth. Culturally mature perspective is unusual in that it values
left-hand and right-hand truths equally. People who recognize limits to
Modern Age extreme archetypally masculine values can be vulnerable
to simply replacing them with ideas that give the archetypally feminine
particular emphasis.
  I noted that when "new paradigm" ideas that address change over time
fall short, most often they have their roots in idealist assumptions. It is an
observation that similarly applies to the thinking of traditional historians,
though there we most often find philosophical idealism of a social as apposed
to spiritual sort. I've described how philosophical idealism views history as
progressing toward some social or spiritual ideal. Hegel's views illustrate
philosophical idealism that posits a social ideal. We find a good example
of philosophical idealism of the more spiritual sort in the early twentieth

This brings us to our second compare-and-contrast approach—looking at differences that have to do not just with how we conceive of change, but that involve how we think about the specific changes that define our time. Most of our stories about what the future holds in store fall into one of two broad categories. In the first group, we find thinking that basically affirms where we have come to, and that for the future assumes the continued viability of the direction that got us here. Such "we've arrived" views acknowledge that there will be bumps in the road ahead—at times, big ones—but they hold that our institutions and our ways of understanding are basically sound. According to these ways of thinking, given time, we can count on our amazing capacities for insight and invention to pull us through whatever difficulties we might face. Their advice for the future: Continue "onward and upward."

Contrasting this first set of beliefs, we find an array of "we've gone astray" views that see culture to be, in some basic way, broken. Extreme examples regard it as irretrievably so, predicting if not a looming Armageddon, at least a world "going to hell in a handbasket." Most such notions offer milder critical interpretations, but all share the assumption that in some fundamental sense, we have failed. They may call, either explicitly or by implication, for going back to some earlier more ideal time. Or they may propose that change of an all-transforming sort provides the only solution.

---

century thinking of **French philosopher and Jesuit priest Teilhard** de Chardin who postulated that history would end at a spiritual enlightenment–like "Omega Point." While people with certain temperaments can find ideas that have roots in spiritual idealism reassuring and inspiring, such thinking ultimately collapses into Unity Fallacy, and thus offers very little that can substantively help us going forward.

To understand philosophical idealism, it helps to think of it in terms of how change is understood in such formulations. Implied in such beliefs is the notion that some "left-hand" force (essence or spirit) drives the "right hand" world of manifest forms (and produces form's realization). A worldview that sees the future in terms of idealized outcomes is the natural result. Creative Systems Theory's developmental/evolutionary picture views left-hand and right-hand sensibilities as playing equal roles in human change processes. This more two-way understanding of change's mechanisms results in Cultural Maturity's less dramatic, more down-to-earth task.

Cultural Maturity's particular developmental/evolutionary interpretation takes us beyond these two more familiar kinds of thinking and puts each in perspective.[49] It makes clear that both positions—the "we've arrived" sort and the "we've gone astray" sort—have problems, certainly in their extremes, but also in more tempered manifestations. Neither kind of story really holds up.

"We've arrived" views fail to recognize that our times require anything that is really new. In contrast, the developmental/evolutionary view we have drawn on emphasizes that there is no reason to conclude that new cultural forms—educational, economic, governmental, scientific, and more—do not lie ahead, and every reason to hope—and assume—that they do. It also emphasizes that few if any of the major challenges ahead can be solved by technological, economic, or policy means alone. Going forward will require not just striving onward, but also changes in how we think, and more deeply, in who we are. The Dilemma of Trajectory puts an exclamation point on this essential conclusion.

The concept of Cultural Maturity agrees with "we've gone astray" interpretations in their assertion that fundamental change is needed. But it sees such interpretations as misunderstanding why change is necessary and putting forth solutions that tend to be, if not dangerous, then at least naïve and ultimately unhelpful. The developmental/evolutionary perspective we have drawn on confronts such conclusions on multiple counts. First, it proposes that most of the conundrums we face today are less the result of error than of our great success as a species. This recognition applies equally to more in-the-world concerns, such as climate change, and to challenges that are more obviously about ourselves, such as the need to address moral questions without the past's one-size-fits-all cultural guideposts. Second, to those who suggest that the task is to somehow return to some supposedly ideal past, the concept of Cultural Maturity makes clear that going back can only be regression and thus solves nothing. And third, to those who argue for radical transformation, it clarifies how

---

49 I say "particular" because this result requires Cultural Maturity's specifically integrative, "second-half" processes. It is possible to have developmental/ evolutionary thinking that does not include such processes.

such advocacy tends to call for outcomes that we could not achieve, and more importantly, that with greater understanding, we would not want to achieve.[50]

Cultural Maturity's notion of a needed and newly possible collective "growing up" argues for a further, entirely different kind of option. It makes clear that going forward as we have can't work as a solution. But at the same time, it emphasizes that the needed change in course is not about correcting past errors (which is not to say that the human enterprise has not involved error), and neither is it about going back. Nor is it about idealized, magical solutions. The concept of Cultural Maturity describes a natural next step in our human development. And it articulates a more explicitly systemic picture both of the challenges ahead and of the possibilities.

A quick summary:

If the analogy between personal maturity and Cultural Maturity holds, Cultural Maturity's changes—at least their potential—are developmentally predicted. We can understand Cultural Maturity in terms of changes not just in *what* we think, but *how* we think—specific cognitive changes. One result of these changes is the capacity for systemic understandings that better reflect that we are alive, and more than this, that we are alive in the particular way that makes us human. Creative Systems Theory uses a creative frame to develop detailed culturally mature concepts. The specific way in which culturally mature perspective views cultural change provides a good tool for separating the wheat from the chaff in our thinking about the human challenges ahead and what these challenges will require of us.

---

50 It also clarifies how most such notions are really not new at all. This is particularly so for advocacy of the more "new age" sort. We have witnessed grand predictions of a coming golden age regularly throughout history. But even interpretations that don't fall for such obviously simplistic conclusions generally reflect either modern day romantic interpretations or new versions of philosophical idealism. Their hopefulness is based on images of transcendence and limitlessness. Cultural Maturity's hopefulness is of an entirely different, more expressly mortal, limits-acknowledging sort.

CHAPTER 7

Looking Ahead—
The Appropriateness of Hope

*Sometimes you have to play for a long time to play like
yourself.*

— MILES DAVIS

Let's conclude by returning to the topic of hope. At the book's
beginning, I asked whether we should be optimistic about the future
and observed that there are good reasons to doubt whether we should
be. The book's reflections have affirmed that concern is justified.

Certainly there are specific concerns. I've described, for example,
how the weapons-of-mass-destruction genie has irretrievably escaped
its bottle. I think there is a good chance that we will again see nuclear
weapons used—possibly by rogue nations, perhaps by terrorists—even
with the most enlightened of policies. I've also emphasized the inex-
cusable harm that will come from continuing to ignore environmental
limits and suggested that it is already too late to avoid significant damage from global climate change. And I've argued that continuing to
think about wealth and progress in the ways that we have before will
result in lives that ever more frequently feel empty, along with increasingly unstable economies.

I've also emphasized more general concerns. My assertion that none
of these challenges can be addressed—or even effectively understood—
without our learning to think and act in fundamentally new ways could
be interpreted as less than encouraging. Thinking and acting in new
ways is no small accomplishment. There is also my troubling list of
Transitional Absurdities. The recognition of how ludicrous we hu-

mans can be could make optimism seem even less warranted. And I've claimed that our contemporary crisis of purpose represents the most ultimately significant of modern concerns. Arguably, it also presents the greatest dangers.

But as should now be clear, the concept of Cultural Maturity ultimately supports hope. At the least, it supports the conclusion that hopeful options are there to be found. It offers a direct answer to my young friend Alex's request that I tell him why "anything we do today really matters." The concept of Cultural Maturity argues that what we do today matters terribly, and not just because we risk calamity, but because our times invite important new possibilities. Possibility does not by itself answer the question of hope. But the simple fact that the idea of a collective "growing up" articulates a way forward is certainly consistent with hope. And the concept of Cultural Maturity goes further to describe how not only does a way forward exist, it's a way forward with rich—indeed profound—implications.

The concept of Cultural Maturity also supports hope by affirming that this way forward is not just some abstract notion or an outcome only to dream about. It provides concrete guidance—describes what a hopeful future requires of us in terms of specific tasks and specific new skills we can learn and practice. All of the new capacities we examined in the book's early chapters—getting beyond projection that leads to conflict, better acknowledging limits, engaging relationships and identity in more complete ways, and thinking of truth and human advancement more systemically—support the effective engagement of Cultural Maturity's challenge. We must be ready for these new capacities if they are to make sense to us. And they don't let us off easily. But if the concept of Cultural Maturity is accurate, they represent accomplishments we are capable of. I've described ways in which many of the most defining achievements of the last century reflect important first steps in the realization of such new, more mature human capacities.

I've also described a characteristic of Cultural Maturity that supports future success with acquiring such capacities: The needed new ways of thinking and acting described by the concept of Cultural Maturity are, as potential, built into who we are. I think it likely that this additional piece is necessary for legitimate optimism. If we needed to invent Cultural Maturity's changes from whole cloth—make them happen simply because they obviously need to happen—hope would be hard to justify. The required leap would be too great. But if the seeds of the needed new capacities lie latent in our makeup, the implications become very different. In that case, what our times ask of us has less to do with radical invention than with garnering the insight and courage needed to make our inherent potential manifest. I've argued that where Cultural Maturity's changes take us is ultimately not obscure or even, in fact, complicated. Consistent with this, when their manifestation is timely, they can feel surprisingly straightforward. This result follows from the fact that the potential for the new skills and capacities that come with Cultural Maturity is inherent in who we are. I've also argued that these are new capacities whose time has come.

The concept of Cultural Maturity also supports hope in a more basic way by offering, simply, that our times are understandable—that however confusing the challenges we face may seem, it is possible for us to make sense of them. It provides a way of thinking about the future that takes us beyond common conflicting views about the tasks ahead. Most obviously important, it challenges views that see the future only in terms of collapse and loss of the familiar. But it also reconciles beliefs that frame the future in more positive, but ultimately limited ways—solely in terms of technological advancement, in terms only of a postmodern multiplicity of options, or in terms of some sudden psychological or spiritual transformation. It provides perspective that is more encompassing—and also, ultimately, more graspable and down to earth. I've described how, while Cultural Maturity's "growing up" requires that we think and act in new ways, in the end it represents "common sense."

The various ways in which Cultural Maturity becomes, in effect, the only viable option we have—in the end, the only game in town—further support clarity. I've observed how it is hard to imagine other avenues by which we might gain the needed new capacities. And the Dilemma of Trajectory makes Cultural Maturity's necessity particularly inescapable. The fact that there is really no fork in the road doesn't guarantee success. It is possible that we could simply lose hope and walk away from it all. But it does sharpen our focus and make the argument for Cultural Maturity—or at least something that can produce related changes—hard to refute.

Can we succeed with what Cultural Maturity asks of us? I find additional encouragement in how, while historically we humans have often hidden from difficult concerns, when we have been given no option but to innovate, we have risen to the demands of seemingly impossible challenges with remarkable consistency. I think the real question going forward is less whether we will see Cultural Maturity's changes, than how much pain we will put ourselves through—and other of the planet's species with us—in the process of getting there. The multiple factors I've listed here support that at least we will get there eventually. And if we are not just potentially capable of what the needed new human maturity asks, but already beginning to make it manifest—as I have suggested—there is yet more reason to assume that given time, we will again rise to the challenge.

I've also observed a further critical way in which the concept of Cultural Maturity is consistent with hope—certainly with the willingness to persevere. It concerns Cultural Maturity's relationship to larger human purpose. If Cultural Maturity were only about survival, the tasks ahead would still justify appropriate diligence. And if it were about survival plus the possibility of a generally healthy and sustainable future, even more deep courage and committed effort would be justified. But Cultural Maturity is about something more fundamental, and fundamentally compelling. It is about a next chapter in our human story of potentially great, indeed profound, importance. Cultural Maturity's new common sense gives our personal lives a whole new depth of meaning. And it gives the human enterprise as a whole a new order of significance. With the recognition of this more fundamental importance, Cultural Maturity stops being only a possibility to learn about and consider, and becomes instead what our times must obviously be about.

Frequently Asked Questions

This brief FAQ summary addresses questions that are often asked by people who are new to the concept of Cultural Maturity.[1]

What is Cultural Maturity?

The concept of Cultural Maturity describes changes that are reordering today's world and further changes that will be necessary if we are to have a healthy and rewarding human future. The concept helps us make sense of why these changes are important, what they ask of us, and how further changes are more likely than we might imagine.

Can you briefly summarize the concept's thesis?

The concept of Cultural Maturity proposes that our times challenge us to engage a critical next stage in our collective human development—put most simply, to engage an essential, and now newly possible, "growing up" as a species. This growing up takes us beyond what has always before been a parent/child relationship between culture and the individual. Cultural Maturity's changes involve leaving behind the protective cultural absolutes of times past and assuming a new level of responsibility in all parts of our lives. They also involve engaging the more demanding and complex—but ultimately more rich and full—kinds of understanding and relating that doing so begins to make possible.

Why do we need such a notion?

Most immediately, the concept of Cultural Maturity provides perspective for making sense of our easily confusing times. It offers a

---

1 A more extensive FAQ summary can be found at www.CulturalMaturity.org.

compelling picture for going forward. It also provides practical guidance for making good decisions in all parts of our personal and collective lives. It helps us delineate the new characteristics that effective thinking, relating, and acting in times ahead must have. In addition, it helps us separate the wheat from the chaff in our ideas about the future and what times ahead will require of us.

What is the evidence that the concept of Cultural Maturity is correct?

Several different kinds of evidence support the concept. Some evidence is empirical. If we list the most critical challenges ahead for the species, we find that effectively addressing them—or even just adequately understanding them—most often requires the greater maturity of perspective that the concept of Cultural Maturity describes. We find further evidence in the way in which many of the most defining advances of the last century have reflected at least first steps toward the new kinds of thinking and relating that the concept of Cultural Maturity predicts.

Additional kinds of evidence are more "developmental." We find that the challenges described by the concept of Cultural Maturity have direct parallels in the tasks that define second-half-of-life developmental changes in our individual lives (and ultimately in the mature stages of any human change process). We can understand Cultural Maturity as a developmentally predicted set of new capacities and realizations.

Some of the most important evidence concerns inescapable realities. Something at least similar to what the concept describes is essential to moving forward for reasons deeper than just the need to effectively address new challenges. It turns out that continuing forward on history's past trajectory is really not an option. Doing so would distance us irretrievably from essential aspects of who we are. Cultural Maturity—or something that can provide a related kind of result—becomes, in effect, the only viable way to proceed.

The concept seems more psychological than most thinking about the future. I guess that makes sense, since you are a psychiatrist. But that seems unusual.

Ultimately the concept of Cultural Maturity concerns the "psyche of culture"—who we are collectively and the particular challenges that today confront us. But there is also a more specifically psychological aspect. Cultural Maturity is not just about various ways of looking at the future, but also about how the particular ways we understand and hold experience affect how we see the future (and also the present and the past). Cultural Maturity involves changes not just in what we think, but how we think—developmentally predicted cognitive changes.

The notion that our times bring into question past culturally specific beliefs sounds a lot like what we hear with postmodern arguments. Is Cultural Maturity just different language for the same kind of conclusion?

The concept of Cultural Maturity begins with some related observations, but in the end it fundamentally challenges—or at least fundamentally extends—the postmodern thesis. Cultural Maturity and postmodern thought similarly bring attention to how our times require us to step beyond culturally defined beliefs. But postmodern perspective does not adequately answer why we should see this challenging of past cultural truths. It also fails to provide much if anything to replace what it quite accurately takes away. The concept of Cultural Maturity specifically addresses why we see the changes we do, and it proposes that the challenge ultimately is not just to surrender past sureties, but to think, relate, and act in some fundamentally new—at once more demanding and more possibility-filled—ways.

You argue that culturally mature perspective requires us to think about social questions more systemically. But you also emphasize that we need to be wary of conceptual traps when using systems language. Could you clarify a bit?

The kind of systems thinking we are most used to is the kind that good engineers draw on. But human questions are not just engineering questions—we are not machines. Culturally mature perspective invites us to think in ways that directly reflect that we are alive—and more than just this, that we are alive in the particular sense that makes us human. If we ignore these needed new steps in our thinking—or misinterpret their implications—we end up with misleading and unhelpful conclusions.

Is Cultural Maturity just another way of talking about the transformations of the Information Age?

There are links. But Cultural Maturity's picture is more encompassing and warns us that thinking in Information Age terms alone can't get us where we need to go. Culturally mature perspective makes clear that very few of the important concerns before us can be resolved solely by technological means. It also challenges the common assumption that invention is the ultimate driver of cultural change. It argues that culture, just as much, shapes what we are able to invent and how we use what we invent. And while much in the information revolution supports Cultural Maturity's changes, much also has the potential to fundamentally undermine culturally mature possibility. If we miss these differences, we can end up pursuing ends that we ultimately would not at all want.

Is Cultural Maturity what people are referring to when they speak of "new paradigm" understanding?

That depends on how a person uses the phrase "new paradigm." The phrase can describe the best of new understanding. But it is also often used to refer to simplistic liberal/romantic, spiritual, or philosophically idealist beliefs masquerading as culturally mature systemic perspective. Such beliefs are not really new. And they tend to advocate for outcomes that would not be possible to achieve and, more to the point, that we would not ultimately want to achieve.

You speak of Cultural Maturity as a simple notion, but it doesn't sound simple to me. Is it or isn't it?

There are ways in which it is simple. It is a single brushstroke notion that we can apply to very different questions. Also, many of Cultural Maturity's underlying characteristics are, in fact, familiar to our experience. We can know a lot about them from the mature stages of other human developmental processes. When such changes at a cultural scale are developmentally timely, we can experience them as surprisingly straightforward. But simple does not mean easy. Cultural Maturity requires us to hold experience with a mature fullness not possible in times past. At the very least, culturally mature perspective requires us to surrender assumptions (often favorite ones) and step into new territories of experience.

Cultural Maturity is a specific concept within Creative Systems Theory's more overarching picture of how human systems grow and change. Do I need to understand Creative Systems Theory to make use of the concept of Cultural Maturity?

No. As a simple metaphor or analogy, the concept of Cultural Maturity works fine as a stand-alone concept. While the concept of Cultural Maturity is a formal Creative Systems Theory notion, there is no need to either understand or agree with the theory's ideas to make effective use of it.

Creative Systems Theory does, however, add to the more basic concept. It helps us understand why Cultural Maturity's challenges are to be expected and exactly what they ask of us. And while all the more nuanced aspects of Cultural Maturity's demands follow directly from Cultural Maturity as a concept, very often the devil is in the details. Creative Systems Theory (though not required) provides simple language for making many of the important distinctions. Creative Systems Theory can also help us think about systems at a level of detail that the concept of Cultural Maturity by itself does not provide.

Creative Systems Theory also has particular significance because it models one successful effort at culturally mature conception. It also represents an approach that can be applied in highly sophisticated ways to a wide variety of questions. But the concept of Cultural Maturity, when understood deeply, requires no support from Creative Systems Theory.

Could you say more about how the concept of Cultural Maturity provides hope for the future?

Most immediately, the concept of Cultural Maturity supports hope by articulating a practical and compelling story for the future. It makes clear that there is very much reason to go on. It also provides specific guidance for going forward—it helps us understand the challenges before us and the capacities needed to effectively engage them. In addition, the concept of Cultural Maturity supports the conclusion that success with the tasks before us is not just some idealized fantasy, or something only in our far-off future. It describes how the potential for the kind of thinking, relating, and acting that the future requires is inherent in who we are. And the fact that many of the most defining advances of the past hundred years reflect the beginnings of culturally mature sensibility supports the conclusion that we are already a good distance on our way—even if we have not had overarching perspective for understanding just what we have been up to.

WORDS OF THANKS

I would like to thank people who, over the years, have played particularly key roles in the development of Creative Systems Theory or who have provided important support in my efforts. In no particular order, my deep appreciation goes out to Larry Hobbs, Rick Jackson, Lyn Dillman, Brenda Kramer, Sandra Wood, Pam Schick, Peggy Hackney, Janice Meaden, Sue Lerner, Dean Elias, Ron Hobbs, Marcy Jackson, Stephen Silha, Steve Boyd, Dona McDonald, Tom Engle, John Palka, Colleen Campbell, David Moore, Dan Senour, and Jeremy Tarcher.

I also wish to give special thanks to my editors Kathy Krause and JoAnne Dyer for their skilled and committed help in making inherently challenging material as clear and accessible as possible, and to Teresa Piddington for help in the proofreading stages. I also want to thank Les Campbell for his beautiful work designing the book's cover, internal layout, and many of its diagrams, and Sayre Coombs for her diagram design artistry.

INDEX

ICD Press is the publishing arm of the Institute for Creative Development. Information about the Institute and other Institute publications can be found on the Institute website www.CreativeSystems.org.

The Institute for Creative Development (ICD) Press
4324 Meridian Ave. N.
Seattle WA 98103
206-526-8562
ICDPressinfo@gmail.com

13891891R00100

Made in the USA
San Bernardino, CA
09 August 2014